By Rocking-Chair
across America

Also by Alex Atkinson & Ronald Searle

★

THE BIG CITY

ALEX ATKINSON
& RONALD SEARLE

By Rocking-Chair
across America

FUNK & WAGNALLS COMPANY
New York

ACKNOWLEDGEMENTS

We are grateful to the proprie-
tors of PUNCH for permission
to reprint the majority of this
material.

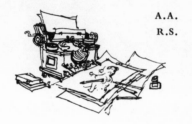

A.A.
R.S.

Contents

INTRODUCTORY NOTE

Too many books about the United States are written by men who have spent only a few weeks in the country. This one is different: it is by a man who has never been there in his life.

Little Old New York

AFTER much thought I chose to enter the United States by way of New York, which quite lived up to my expectations. It proved to be a thriving city largely situated on a small island off the coast of New Jersey, containing Grant's tomb and The Polo Grounds.

I had decided that this town would probably be a fairly convenient jumping off place for a tour of the country, since it is connected to the mainland by a ferry service and several short bridges, each of which is the longest in the world. In point of fact, when the time came for me to say good-bye to New York and strike out into the U.S.A. proper I hired a small boat from a humble clam-fisher whose grandfather was born in County Mayo, and rowed across the picturesque Harlem River to Third Avenue. From here it was but a stone's throw to Hartford and the grim wastes of the Appalachian Mountains, dotted with lonely commuters' shacks and the nests of bald-headed eagles.

But I am rushing ahead. Let me deal with New York.

(That's the trouble with the U.S.A., especially down the right-hand side: the sense of urgency, which comes sweeping across the country in the prevailing wind from Portland, Oregon, seizes you like a fever, so that you frequently find yourself half-way through to-morrow's schedule before you've digested yesterday's tranquillizer. I met one well-to-do business-man, a manufacturer of psychiatrists' sundries, who actually keeps his desk-calendar a week ahead of anybody else's. " Nobody's going to steal a march on me, Mac," he explained. On one wall of his office there was a sign which read: " It's Too Late Already," and he told me that he had started excavations for a deep shelter before the ink was properly dry on Einstein's Theory of Relativity.)

New York, then. First, the historical background. To begin with, the

Dutch, rather surprisingly, were persuaded to buy the place from the aborigines for some beads they happened to have, and later the British introduced street-lighting. The cosmopolitan atmosphere was further enhanced by the erection in the harbour of a monument to the French Revolution and the arrival of practically all the inhabitants of Ireland. The latter, having established themselves in Tammany Hall, proceeded to lay the foundations of the police force, the Notre Dame football team, and Errol Flynn. So the city grew, until to-day it is the headquarters of the Delta Phi Epsilon Sorority, with a mean annual temperature of 54 degrees, legalised Bingo, and a brisk trade in boots and shoes.

Never shall I forget my first sight of the Manhattan skyline. I had seen nothing quite like it since I watched the Liver Building fade from view as we slipped down the Mersey, with the majestic derricks of the renowned Birkenhead shipyards silhouetted dramatically against the sunset away to starboard, and Bootle's biscuit factories pointing their fantastic chimney-fingers to the sky on the right. The Statue of Liberty, too, I found impressive. It is a big effigy of Frederic Auguste Bartholdi's mother, with people walking round her hat for ten cents.

I asked my guide (his name was Pilsudski, and his grandmother was born in County Mayo) whether he would mind if I took a snapshot of the statue. (I had to ask him, because he was standing in my way.) " Listen, Mac," he said kindly. " I know it must seem strange to you, but here you can go *any* place, see *any*thing, take all the pictures you *want*, and no questions asked. You know why? Because this ain't no Welfare State, that's why."

I could see by the elephant in his lapel that he was a Republican.

I encountered no difficulty with the immigration people once I had signed a confession, although they kept me waiting rather a long time while they examined the three pages of *New Statesman* which I always fold up inside the headband of my hat when I've had a haircut. They didn't make any comment, but later on I noticed men with big shoulders lurking behind pillars as I signed in at my hotel, eyeing me expressionlessly over the tops of their *New York Herald-Tribunes*. Under their armpits they had suspicious-looking lumps. One was flipping a coin. I strolled over to him.

" Look, Mac," I said, " My father was born in County Mayo."

He batted an eyelid. " In a pig's eye," he said.

All the same, he and his companions (or " buddies," as they say in New York) presently left, rather sheepishly, and drove off in a bullet-proof sedan. I had won the first round.

Reaching my hotel room I found that it had been systematically searched, and a small tape-recorder placed under the bed. I smiled to myself, enigmatically.

The hotel itself was just off Broadway, and therefore inclined to be noisy. Each day at about dawn I would be awakened by the sound of Follies girls being rolled home along the corridors by laughing Shriners in evening dress and cardboard fezzes, on account of a Convention. Apart from that, I liked the place. It had a friendly atmosphere. The lift-boys treated you as an equal. You felt that you *belonged*. Then again, you didn't have to go very far before you found an ice-water machine, and often I would join some merry group as they gathered at one of these oases for a few minutes' light-hearted banter, pounding one another on the back and making their wild Indian calls as they quenched their thirsts from little paper cups. There were laundries, swimming-pools, cinemas, rehabilitation centres and, in the room next to mine, a poker-game that had been in progress since 1951. On the other hand the tea was beyond words—and so, for that matter, was the coffee.

During those first few magical nights I would listen to the sounds of the city after dark as I lay in bed on the eighty-second floor; the eerie wailing of sirens as the cops drove relentlessly about their precincts wearing grey fedoras; the intermittent yelping of stabbed delinquents from over towards Central Park; the rattle of the window-cleaners' buckets as they hung like spiders on the Empire State Building, performing their never-ending task; the unmistakable clang of a spittoon being kicked over somewhere far below; the sobs of the maladjusted as they tramped the streets in search of an analyst with a night-bell; the weird metallic sounds as lovers and undesirable aliens tapped out messages on the central-heating pipes; an occasional thud as the latest edition hit the street; the soft murmur of conversation floating up from the sun-baked stoops of brownstone houses as the citizens took their ease in T-shirts, sneakers and Bermuda shorts, smoking a last cigar and exchanging homespun philosophy under the garish neon signs; the purposeful footsteps of Walter Winchell and Drew Pearson echoing through the silent streets and alleys as they kept their fingers on the pulse of this great metropolis; now and then a muffled roar as G-men turned their powerful flame-throwers on a crop of marijuana growing in secret on some vacant lot; the steady drone from the apartments of a thousand immigrant Puerto Ricans as they slept with their TV sets full on; the swish of call-girls speeding through the night in convertibles on their errands of mercy; and, beneath it all, as a constant reminder of New York's buoyant gaiety, the gales of full-throated laughter

drifting up from the Main Stem—the jolly voice of the Great White Way itself—as the merrymakers surged along from Trinity Church to West 261st Street in a never-ending carnival procession, blowing squeakers, drinking from hip-flasks, discussing the latest play, getting vitamins out of slot-machines, meeting college chums, pouring in and out of happy clip-joints, and proving to the world at large that this is still the most joyful street on earth, or even in America.

Unhappily, when I saw Broadway in the daytime it seemed to be closed.

I believe a short account of my host in New York might not be inappropriate here. Like most New Yorkers he was in advertising (the remainder work in the garment district), and he wore such big shoes that he walked like a man with fallen arches. (Actually his arches were in good repair. What he chiefly feared was athlete's foot.) He had entered the advertising profession against his will, his father having unfortunately known an influential man called Ed. He gave me to understand that it was a rat race. All the senior office-boys (or vice-presidents as they are called) hated one another bitterly; each one of them would go to extreme lengths to get himself a private office with his very own ice-water machine, caring little who got stomach ulcers in the process. Gil (my host) had three times been hauled before his acting supreme president-in-chief to answer charges of yawning at the American flag in a subway, knowing a man called Stalin, refusing to eat green ice-cream on St. Patrick's Day, and other un-American activities. He owned nothing in the world except a tube of Helthi-Gumm toothpaste (" Gets Gums *Really* White ") and a cigarette-lighter inscribed *To a Great Guy, from the Boys in the Corner Drugstore*. Everything else was on credit. His grandfather was born in County Mayo, and he lived in a Colonial-style brownstone walk-up duplex penthouse apartment with a built-in bar, two air-conditioned rumpus rooms (His and Hers), and an uninterrupted view of a tree in Brooklyn. He had two children, one female and mentally stable, one male and emotionally disturbed. They were aged five and six respectively. His wife was organizing secretary of the local branch of the American Mothers' League for the Furtherance of Modern Shakespearean Research and Netball. She had her own convertible and was being treated for schizophrenia. " I have only the mildest form," she told me. " I think I must have caught it at Coney Island. I go for observation each Tuesday, with the woman next door. She's *much* worse, on account her husband isn't properly integrated, the dope."

Their son, who was tall for six and rather inclined to flabbiness, organized the life of the whole family single-handed, choosing their clothes, their food, their entertainment, the order in which they took showers, and the subjects for their after-dinner conversation. His advice was sought on everything from finance to family planning, and if anybody dared to doubt the wisdom of any of his decisions he would set fire to the linen-cupboard, rush out into the night, and terrorize the neighbourhood with a steak-knife which he'd sharpened to a fine point. His little sister had a home perm once a week, and used a slightly paler shade of lipstick than her mother. When she grew up she was going to be a hostess on a quiz show. Neither she nor her brother had a convertible.

"We all get along just fine," Gil said. "After all, you have to have *some* kind of discipline."

Each year they spend a few weeks in their summer place—a prefabricated log cabin in the Adirondacks with a deep-freeze and a fully equipped cinema for showing home movies. ("When we're at home we can see ourselves playing ball in the Adirondacks, and when we're in the Adirondacks we can see ourselves playing ball in Central Park.") Here they hunt for bears, catch catfish, and swap yarns around a communal Eezi-Bild campfire with friends and business associates from back home who also have log cabins. "I guess it's the pioneer instinct," Gil said. "Every time I unpack the folding chromium barbecue kit and the dehydrated soup mix, out there under the stars, I say to myself, 'Gil, boy, this is something you can't escape: it's in your blood.' I guess every New Yorker would willingly trade his convertible for a covered wagon, if only there was some place to go."

I met many men like Gil during my stay in New York, and I'm sure that if I'd been there a little longer I might have learned to tell a few of them apart.

As to the city itself, it has left a lasting impression on me. I shall not easily forget Times Square, where the man-in-the-street congregates so that television inquirers can get his views on the world situation; nor Greenwich Village, where the Paris of the 'twenties is nostalgically preserved. I shall remember the busiest port in the world, the second longest tunnel, the tallest building, the thinnest woman, the best-known boxing arena, the greatest baseball team, the best-stocked zoo, the largest natural harbour, and the biggest shop.

But perhaps most of all I shall remember the taxi-driver who, when I told him that you can't fool all of the people all of the time, replied, "That's right, Mac: but we're working on it."

I Reach the Mainland

IT is surprising how quickly one can get used to having mayonnaise poured over one's bacon and egg. I had been in the United States no more than two weeks (or a fortnight, as we say in England) when I found myself wolfing down this exotic dish like a native. The absence of a knife tended to slow me up at first, but no eyebrows were raised when I took to scooping up the heavy juice with my tea-spoon. I am confident that if ever I get to San Francisco I'll be able to tackle my porridge with chop-sticks as to the manner born.

I cannot deny that I find *all* American food exciting. By the time I reached Rhode Island (the smallest state in the Union, famous for red hens and the Woonsocket worsted plants) I had tried tinned apricots in mutton stew, tomato sauce on trifle (with pistachio nuts), strawberry jam with a double-decker sandwich of home-cured pork and crayfish, and lamb chops swimming in chocolate sauce. The great thing about Americans, leaving aside their plumbing for the moment, is that they are not *afraid* of their food. They are also, of course, justly proud of their seltzer industry.

Curiously enough, I never caught the habit of dipping my cake in my coffee and sucking lumps off it. My American friends put this down to the quaint English passion for drawing the line, and I suppose they were right. There are, after all, limits.

New England is up in the top right-hand corner—about as far away from wicked Las Vegas as it can get without actually putting out to sea. It is very old and slightly more historic than Stratford-on-Avon, Warwickshire. I was constantly being shown bits of the *Mayflower*, scenes of bloody massacres by the British, genuine pilgrims' hats marked *Kiss Me Baby*, or the graves of people like Hawthorne, Tom Thumb, Samuel Adams and Louisa May Alcott. In Boston, Mass., which is a place of interest in New England (others being

Wiscasset, Skowhegan and the Jethro Coffin House in Nantucket, admission
30c.), I saw the place where Emerson grazed his mother's cow. It seemed
an ideal spot. Here too I saw where Paul Revere, a rider, finally crushed the
armed might of Britain with a lantern and some Minute Men; and outside
the Boston Athenæum (closed Sat.) an old gentleman with bean-stains on his
necktie told me that the planet Jupiter rises five minutes earlier in Boston
than it does in Washington. I congratulated him warmly, and made a mental
note to see what the position is in Texas. The conversation then taking a
more personal turn, he revealed that he suffered on and off from attacks of
split personality, owing to the fact that while his grandmother was born in
County Mayo like everybody else, he was saddled with three earlier ancestors
who were first, second and third ashore respectively at Plymouth on December
16th, 1620. When I suggested that this made the shape of his family tree seem
wildly improbable, he drew himself up to his full height and said that still another
of his relations had put his name to Magna Carta. Not only that, but he had
trained men hard at work that very moment in London, England, trying to count
up how many Angles, Saxons, and Jutes there were on his mother's side.
" And this," he said, showing me his waistcoat, " is the family tartan."

Since it is nice and handy, and more historic than Yale, all the young men
of Boston go to Harvard, where many of the books they are encouraged to
read would stand a fair chance of being publicly burned back in their old home
town. To counterbalance this, and possibly as a precaution, co-eds are not
allowed. Longfellow was a professor at Harvard, and one likes to think that
T. S. Eliot first came under his influence when he studied there. One also
likes to think of T. S. Eliot roaring around the campus in a Model T Ford,
with a capital H on his sweat-shirt, singing " Ain't She Sweet." The Harvard
boys make a gay picture as they roam the autumn woods waving football
pennants, quoting bits of *Walden,* and blushing at the young ladies from
Radcliffe College. (New England is divided, by the way, into the Autumn
Tints Zone and the Breughel Territory. There are two separate sets of
weather conditions, which remain constant: nobody, for example, ever saw
Vermont under less than three feet of snow, with honest puritan Yankees
plodding grimly to church in all directions; while Massachusetts woods
somehow contrive to grow in a perpetual blaze of fall splendour.)

Maine is bigger than any other New England state, and has more sardines.
Its inhabitants also vote two months earlier than anybody else in the Union—
not because they are impatient but because the whole world knows they're going
to vote Republican anyway, so they figure they might as well get it over with and

go on planting potatoes. I took the opportunity of penetrating to the northern border of Maine, accompanied by a man in a fur hat and snowshoes who happened to be going that way, and before I knew where I was we were in Canada.

I found the Canadians very friendly, all three of them. They spoke fluent French with a Scottish acent, and had Union Jacks in cupboards at home, but apart from that they were indistinguishable from other Americans. There were *superficial* differences, of course, but I was assured that these are being ironed out all the time. I believe it's the same in Australia. Presently, steering the conversation away from mink-trapping and the putting of middle-cut salmon into cans, I inquired about the progress of the arts in Canada, and was delighted to learn that they now have two or three theatres. " I don't —how you say?—*go* much for it myself," my informant told me, " but, hoots, I guess it's something for the women-folk, yes? "

New Hampshire is different. The Algonquins ran it at one time, and seem to have been happy enough, while in the town of Newport *Mary Had a Little Lamb* was written. In Franklin I was able to see the homestead of Daniel Webster for a quarter. I had a long chat about the great man with my guide, and it wasn't until a week later (or a sennight, as we say) that I realized I had been talking about Daniel Boone all the time.

" So then," said my guide, " Dan'l he ups and tells Senator Hayne, ' Liberty and Union,' he says, ' now and forever, one and inseparable'. "

" Ah, yes," I said. " That would be just before he was captured by the Shawnee Indians."

I wasn't *too* embarrassed about this, because the ignorance of some Americans about *our* country is quite staggering. I was actually to meet a woman, in Detroit of all places, who didn't know that a Number 13 bus goes to Swiss Cottage.

New Hampshire is a busy little state. Wherever I went they seemed to be up to something—making wood pulp, quarrying granite, catching lobsters, digging up gneiss, or manufacturing cotton goods. There are still quiet parts, of course, where the true New England atmosphere prevails. In such places one is often reminded of home—thatched cottages, housing estates, soft-drink ads, leafy lanes and bubble-gum machines: but there the resemblance ends, for the people seem quite foreign, They are starchy, unbending, secretive, dark-clad and religious. How I missed the familiar sound of laughing British crowds!—the smiling faces on every hand, the open-hearted chatter on the Underground, the readiness to exchange confidences with total strangers, the brilliant flashes of colour from the women's beige overcoats, the light-hearted bowlers of the men! Here I found only silent groups all dressed in grey and

black, who stood in the streets and stared at me suspiciously, holding pitch-forks and Nonconformist hymn-books.   When I asked the way in a place in Vermont the village green emptied in an instant, except for an old woman with a besom who went on oiling the stocks.   Shutters banged across all the windows, and I was aware of beady eyes watching me through chinks.   These, I reflected, were the people who declared war on Nazi Germany before the United States got around to it, and I didn't find it hard to believe.

They are famous in Vermont for milk and marble, and on the side they make very sinister things indeed, like portable ovens and electronic organs.   When they have a parade the drum-majorettes wear hobble skirts.   They use only one word at a time, like Gary Cooper, and it usually means No.   If it doesn't mean No it means Why.   The women part their hair in the middle, and the men wear collars only on a Sunday.   When I asked them what they thought of Britain they narrowed their eyes and began collecting jagged stones. Appropriately enough it was Emerson who said there should always be a minority unconvinced.   It lives in Vermont.

The world's biggest watch factory is in New England somewhere, but I never got around to it, what with fishing for square-tail and horned pout, shooting duck, picking cranberries, grappling with swordfish, playing possum, skiing, and trying to find Thoreau's hut.   What an exciting part of the world this is!   They make submarines in Connecticut, and produce more scallops and abrasive garnets in Massachusetts than anywhere else on earth.   In Massachusetts, too, the inventor of the spring bed was actually born.   And yet, apart from all this feverish activity, there are places like Narragansett, Rhode Island, where rich New Yorkers loll and browse in their palatial summer residences, planning their winter sales campaigns; artists' colonies on the coast of Maine where fat old ladies in floppy hats and striped shorts paint yachts and argue about Grandma Moses and Modigliani; authors' colonies where young men barely out of their first convertibles lie about in the sun threatening to write longer books than James Gould Cozzens; sculptors' colonies, madrigal colonies, fretwork colonies, and a colony devoted to a systematic study of the printer's errors in *Finnegans Wake*.   New England is in fact a cradle of the arts.

In 1701 Yale was started in New Haven, Conn., because Harvard found they had no one to play football with.   Since then Yale has never looked back, and now has a Glee Club and a brontosaurus skeleton seventy feet long. When I had seen this I went to Pennsylvania.

I visited Niagara Falls on the way.   This involved a detour, but it was worth it: never in my life have I seen a larger source of power for electro-

metallurgy.   As a spectacle it is rather noisy by comparison with Stonehenge, but the honeymoon facilities are far more elaborate.   For 90c. including waterproof clothing you can sail to the foot of the thing and frighten yourself to death.   " They ain't got nothing like this in Limehouse, Mac! " the guide yelled proudly.   " I only have your word for that! " I shouted back.   Next day, having ascertained that there were no arrangements for anyone to cycle across on a tightrope, I left for Philadelphia, Penn.

Pennsylvania turned out to be almost as historic as New England.   (I have reached the conclusion that if Americans have something that isn't *taller* than anything else it had better be *older* or they'll tear it down and sell it.)   I saw the Liberty Bell (free), Edgar Allan Poe's house (50c.) and the chair where people sat to sign the Declaration of Independence.   All this was in Philadelphia, but in Pittsburgh they seem to go in for making steel.   Pennsylvania is a mixed-up state altogether.   For instance, one day you might run into a crowd of Amish people walking about without any buttons, and the next day you might find yourself in a country-club district, where everybody knows everybody else and can't understand how in the world they can afford to keep two convertibles *and* a British car.   These are mostly commuters, of the same type as those to be found in parts of N.Y.   One night they have a party of their own, and the next night they go to a party up the street, and so on.   In this way they manage to see the same people every night, but against a different décor.   It makes them feel that they *belong*.   A party is a good deal of gin, less vermouth, and a lot of kidding about infidelity.   Occasionally there is a divorce, or a suicide, and so far *Reader's Digest* hasn't been able to find a solution to it all.   They are inclined to blame the *New Yorker*, but they think it will work out all right in the end.

I have, like Stephen Vincent Benét before me, fallen in love with American names.   On the night before I left Pa. and struck out boldly into the interior I lay tossing and turning in my brownstone motel on the border of W. Va., listening to the kidnappers crunching up in their stolen convertibles to change licence-plates and hear the latest radio reports of their progress.   And all night long the wild, romantic place-names clanked majestically through my head, beckoning, tempting, irresistible . . .

> *Clinton, Clanton, Claxton, Scranton,*
> *Hamtramck, Hackensack, Harrogate, Cocoa;*
> *Dickeyville, Bradford, Soap Lake, Nitro,*
> *Mechanicsville, Murphy, Marblehead, Henderson. . . .*

I have also made a note to visit What Cheer, Iowa.

Splendid Isolation

I AM bound to say that at the outset the Middle West was something of a disappointment to me, because it turned out to be in the north.

To make matters worse, according to my calculations it lies a little to the east and quite a distance from the middle, which is in Kansas—or was, until Alaska threw everything into confusion. (Of course, there are inhabitants of Kansas who claim they're Middle West anyway, but you'll *always* find people who want to get in on the act, and it shouldn't be encouraged. Once you admit Kansas, before you know where you are you'll have New Mexico hammering at the door, and the thing will become farcical.)

On the whole I believe it would be more accurate to call the Middle West the Middle East, if anything, and I suggested this to a man in Oshkosh. He went on manufacturing truck axles for a few minutes and then he said " That don't alter the fact that Edna Ferber was born in Wisconsin." You can't argue with men in Oshkosh, and that also goes for men in Lawrenceburg, Indiana, where they make buggies for Hollywood. (" Why are you making all these buggies, neighbour? " I asked this man in Lawrenceburg. " For Hollywood," said the man. " Do they use a lot of buggies, then, in Hollywood? " I asked. " I don't know what they do with them," said the man, " but they sure seem crazy about 'em, and that's good enough for me.")

Dust-stained, smelling of hot rubber and sheep-dip, with alfalfa seeds in my hair and my convertible ankle-deep in peanut-shells, I reached the Middle West after driving for about three weeks in a dead straight line along a highway, stopping only for gas, water, hot-dogs, gophers, highway patrols, road-blocks, landslides, stick-ups, floods, free air and unfenced cattle. It is a region of contrasts: in one Main Street you might see a boy wearing baseball boots and a space-helmet, while in another you might not. Chances are you will, though. It is also a region of isolationism, because its people are trapped. On the whole they don't complain about this, but the fact remains that they are hemmed in, probably for ever—by a lot of lakes and the Dominion of Canada to the north, by the Rockies to the west, by the Alleghenies to the east, and by the hill-billies to the south. (Some reckless spirits have in the past tried to pioneer an escape route down through Kentucky, only to find themselves nailed to barn-doors or held captive in the mountains and worshipped as mysterious ju-ju men.) To many Midwesterners, therefore, the outside world remains an enigma, and a pretty mixed-up one at that. They regard Charleston as just an old-time dance, Lebanon as simply a town in either Indiana or Missouri. Lebanon means nothing more to them: they don't know about Lebanon Oregon, Lebanon Penn., Lebanon Vermont, or even Lebanon Tennessee. And in a little place in Minnesota I didn't cause the slightest ripple of excitement when I put down my nationality as Zulu in the hotel register. The hotel clerk was the only one who showed any interest. He asked me if we were still pestered with kangaroos in China, and told the chef to rustle up some astrakhan for my supper. To give them their due, however, I found that many Midwesterners know about England. England is where the British live. The British roam around constantly in their gunboats colonizing defenceless people. They are chiefly remarkable in that they flatly refuse to pay their War Debts.

A maker of steel wagon beds near Chillicothe, Missouri, where Sloan's Liniment was invented in 1870, told me that a good many Midwesterners wouldn't have picked the Middle West as a place to live if they'd had a choice. "The way I figure it," he said, "it all came about by accident. In the old days most everybody from the east was heading out to California, and it just so happened that round about half-way they hit the Middle West, and a lot of wagons broke down. So some folks said 'The hell with it, we ain't in no fit condition to do a repair job on this here old wagon, we might as well stay right here.' And they did. So they became our ancestors, and if it hadn't been for that this whole place might still be Cherokee country to-day, same as Oklahoma, and I ain't saying it wouldn't have been an improvement, at that."

He was being modest, of course, for there are splendid things to see in the Middle West, what with wall-eyed pike in the Ozarks, the University of Minnesota, the grave of War Eagle, the Home of ex-President Truman, and one hundred and forty varieties of hybrid lilacs in the Nichols Arboretum, Ann Arbour, Michigan (free, open daily 9 to 9). There is also Ohio, if it

Ronald Searle

comes to that; where they make soap, tables, false teeth, wine and playing-cards, and where, in the town of Tiffin, Heidelberg College was founded in 1850. Ohio is also notorious for the number of presidents it has produced. There were seven in all, and they were all Republicans. Two were shot dead, and one was Warren G. Harding. There are more Methodists in Columbus than you'd think possible, and I met a girl student at Ohio State University who was taking courses in Old Provençal and Ice Cream Manufacturing.

I spent enough time in a typical small Midwestern town to be able to form a vivid impression of the place. It has a population of nearly four thousand, of whom a hundred and fifty are dentists. It lies in the midst of a vast, empty plain: you could tear south down the highway some evening at eighty miles an hour (in your convertible) and it would be no more than a flurry of lights as you passed it, or a snatch of Frank Sinatra on a juke-box. On Main Street there are four pediatricians, five drug-stores, three morticians, one chain-store, one corn chandler's, four churches, a temple, two super-markets, two movie theatres, five bars, three used-car marts, two banks and a wooden Indian. This is the centre of the town, and the gaily coloured convertibles make a pleasant sight parked four deep at each side of the street while the people who are gradually paying for them go about their business or pleasure on every hand. Here are fashionable matrons trudging along to rest their feet in beauty parlours after a hard morning entertaining some visiting celebrity at a pre-lecture *soirée* (ninety-seven guests in their very best rhinestones, plus one husband to mix the drinks). Here are two corpulent, beringed gentlemen with hula girls painted gaily on their ties. They are fanning themselves with their sharkskin trilbies as they pause for a democratic chat with a humble newsvendor under the plane trees. They are running for mayor, and so is he. Here is a bunch of kids, swinging along happily from the nearest vacant lot with bats, balls, gloves, and gum, singing some quaint American folk-song as they turn in to the Happi Phun Parlor to play the fruit machines before going home to television. Here is another bunch, thundering down the street like bats out of hell in their sawn-off hot-rods, scattering the quick and the dead. Here is another bunch, in black leather jackets slightly old-fashioned by New York standards, shuffling menacingly up the street with their hands in their pockets and their faces pudgy, eyeless, identical. Are they on their way to a lynching? To dancing-class? To finish their homework? There is no way of telling. Here is the man who runs the town, tossing away half a cigar as he elbows aside the shirt-sleeved cop on the corner and strolls

into a barber-shop to investigate some discrepancy in last week's taking on the horses. Here is the editor of the local paper, hurrying out of his office wearing a green eye-shade, to snatch a hasty ham on rye with dill pickle, ketchup and mustard before finishing his fearless leading article on graft in the sanitation department. Altogether it makes a lazy, comfortable picture in the sunlight—a shining example to the underdeveloped nations of the world.

But let us take a look at the residential area. Here there are rows of desirable real estate units, each with a garage and a wife and a kitchen full of chromium gadgets with plastic handles. (There are more gadgets in general use in the Middle West than anywhere else in the world, because during the long months of winter, with the Country Club cut off by snow-drifts and the Mississippi rising ominously and cyclones tossing telegraph poles about like matches and the local psychiatrist on his annual vacation in Florida, there's not much left to do except leaf through the Sears Roebuck catalogue, and if you can't find a gadget in that to suit any activity known to man or beast, there's always Montgomery Ward's.) Each desirable real estate unit also has a front garden, across which the papers are flung every morning by a freckle-faced kid working his way through college, and a back-yard. On long summer evenings the back-yard becomes the living-room, which is why nearly all American plays are set in the Middle West: it's so easy to get people on and off the stage. Neighbours drop by with pots of home-made preserves. The daft old auntie from next door but one drifts to and fro in a sprigged muslin frock, saying " Land sakes! " and fluttering her hands like Zasu Pitts. Moths flicker in the fading light. Pa sits in a rocker trying to concentrate on the funnies while Junior upbraids him for not giving him something to hold on to, something so he'll know where he belongs, so he won't all the time be forced to go around getting into scrapes, like this business now where he had to shoot this cop on account of not being properly orientated motivation-wise and nobody *understanding*. Ma smiles her deep smile, sitting on the porch step mending socks and dreaming of the days when she was the belle of the Golf Club's Grand Annual Dance and Spare Rib Supper three years running. Little daughter sits under the sour-apple tree trying to make her mouth fall open like Brigitte Bardot's without showing the gap in her teeth, while the boy from up the street wonders how he's going to tell her that he's already given his fraternity pin to Lizzie, whose ma *does* let her wear a sweater. Cousin Hiram leans against a post, picking his teeth as he reminisces about the great time he had himself at the State Fair, what with his hog winning a second prize and all, and the country girls going plumb crazy to be his partner in the square-dancing, and him drinking so much apple-jack he sang a song that made most everybody laugh fit to bust, and the coconut shies and the Fat Lady and the crowning of the State Fair Queen of 1921 and all. Grandpa mooches about with his braces dangling, cursing the Maybugs and wondering why the local horse-doctor hasn't shown up yet for a game of pinochle. Big daughter snuggles down in the elderberry bushes with the mysterious handsome stranger who hit town three days ago and already has all the women's heads in a whirl. "My," she sighs, "but you resemble William Holden *greatly*."

Chekhov would have loved the Middle West.

There are, of course, big cities in the region, and among these I was anxious to see Detroit, long famous for adding-machines, convertibles and garden seeds, and Chicago, which, apart from the *Tribune,* boasts an aluminium statue of the goddess Ceres on top of its Board of Trade building, weighing six tons. They both turned out to be lively enough cities, but Chicago in particular was draughty.

At close quarters Detroit was a quaint, seething nightmare of blast furnaces, picket-lines, race riots, and a genuine Cotswold cottage. You can hear the city roaring twenty miles away, and see it belching smoke and flames. Twenty miles away is a good place to be, at that. I don't suppose Henry Ford himself would have stayed there five minutes if he hadn't had some crazy notion that his new-fangled automobiles would catch on.

In Chicago I saw very little of the underworld gangs (or Trade Unions, as they are now called), but there was some sporadic shooting as I drove north on State Street, that great street, and in the burlesque houses, strip shows, honky tonks and other dens of iniquity which abound to ensnare the gullible traveller (I must have visited at least thirty) I thought I caught sight of some gorillas, mugs, goons, hatchet-men, footpads and politicians from time to time, but I couldn't be sure, because Chicago citizens tend to look alike. I put this down to the fact that in the process of evolution down the years from the Prohibition Age they have gradually developed protective colouring. You mustn't think, however, that Chicago is only notable for tinned meat and massacres. I found, among other things, that it has the world's largest collection of meteorites, a river that runs backwards, a museum containing both a German U-boat and a full-size working coal-mine (adm. 25c. each), two statues of Abraham Lincoln (one standing, one sitting) and a college of dentistry.

It was Chicago, by the way, that had the fire—not San Francisco.

Up the Airy Mountain

WHEN, in the course of human events, it becomes necessary for one people to dissolve the political bands which have connected them with another, and to assume among the powers of earth the separate and equal station to which the Laws of Nature and of Nature's God entitle them, you've got to expect some pretty rum developments. For instance (and leaving aside the question as to which side of the road Nature intended a convertible to be driven on), the farther I travel the more often I am impressed by the relentless appetite for *facts* which characterizes the majority of America's 173,210,000 inhabitants.

On my way to the Northwestern States, to take a case in point, I fell into conversation with a man from Spokane. It was in a typical roadside diner made out of a disused observation-car from the Chicago, Indianapolis and Louisville Railroad, gay with the chatter of hunters in check shirts and fur hats, migratory lumberjacks, travelling salesmen, and fully paid-up members of the International Brotherhood of Teamsters, Chauffeurs, Warehousemen and Helpers of America. As we munched our fried eggs, burgers, sauerkraut, and hold the gravy, watching an American League basket-ball game on the television and listening to non-stop mountain music on the juke-box, the man from Spokane first softened me up by giving me some account of the joys and heartaches of his formative years. Over the coffee and Monsta Doh-Knuts (" They're *Ventilated!* ") he added a few vivid word-pictures of his kinfolk and acquaintances and illustrated these by snapshots, press-cuttings, love letters and other documentary evidence. Then he worked gradually into a half-hour résumé of the formidable and complicated forces which had combined to put his marriage on the rocks and involve him in an entanglement with this Evelyn woman, the one with the old man in cement and no idea of the value of money.

At last, the preliminaries out of the way, he settled down to plunder me of statistics. His persistence was so great that despite my native reserve I was finally prevailed upon to admit the existence of a vague possibility that I might have been born, not to put too fine a point on it, in a place not a thousand leagues away from Liverpool. It was enough. His notebook was out in a flash. The tears were gone from his eyes, his voice was crisp. How far in land miles was Liverpool from Weston-super-Mare? From Stratford-on-Avon? From the Horse Guards Parade? How many telephones did it have in 1958, *per capita?* In 1939? What was the known height in feet and inches of the City Hall? The weight, in pounds? What were the mean annual precipitation figures? What was the city motto; in Latin? In English? The name of the sheriff or other responsible officer? How many dry-goods stores? What was the incidence of hay fever? How many rural homes without toilet or privy? Which way did Liverpool vote? What was it doing about soil erosion? And so on.

I gave my answers readily enough, and it is my firm belief that encounters of this kind must play a considerable part in fostering the suspicions and misapprehensions which so often and so regrettably cloud the relations between our two countries. There must by now be scores of people in and near Spokane for instance (and heaven knows how much further the poison has spread) who hold these truths to be self-evident, that there were 20,040 adult males in Liverpool with only one decent pair of trousers as of last July, and that the Goodison Park football stadium seats 100,000 people.

Be that as it may, I must now report my findings on the Great Pacific Northwest, which has changed since two men in canoes called Lewis and Clark stumbled across it around 1805, but not much, unless you want to count Seattle. Is was in the state of Washington (state capital Olympia, state flower Rhododendron, maximum speed 50 m.p.h.) that I saw my first grizzled prospector. He was crouching near the Blewett Pass in the Wenatchee Mountains, at an altitude of 4,071 ft., give or take an inch, at 4 p.m. Pacific Standard Time (eight bells). He had a panhandle in one hand and a pemmican sandwich in the other. When he wasn't stuffing gold-dust into his poke he was feeding crumbs to the rattlers which played about his feet like puppy-dogs. Seeing me, he waved a friendly greeting, and snatching up a small-bore double-barrelled flintlock Winchester repeating rifle, drilled a hole in my bowler from a distance of fifty yards. Visibility was moderate.

I won his confidence by calling him Pardner, and we soon became the best of friends. Apart from being grizzled, he was ornery. He also had horny hands, and his eyes were like slits. He chawed tobacco. (He showed me how to do this: it is like chewing, only slower.)   In his pouch he carried a daguerreotype of his old mother (she was born in County Wexford, for some reason), a few lucifers for lighting fires, a bowie knife, and a crumpled map marked with crosses where he figured there was gold.   His wide-brimmed hat served to keep the sun off his weather-beaten face.   After sundown he used it as a cooking-pot.   In thirty years of prospecting he had accumulated close on twenty-seven and fourpence-worth of the precious dust that sets men's brains aflame.   " But it ain't just the gold that matters," he told me: " it's the fever. Once you strike it rich you're heading for trouble.   You no doubt recall the immortal lines of Robert W. Service, born in Preston, Lancashire?—

> *They're making my money diminish:*
> *I'm sick of the taste of champagne.*
> *Thank God! when I'm skinned to a finish*
> *I'll pike to the Yukon again.*

Course, this here ain't exactly the Yukon, but Service sure knowed all the answers.   By hominy, some of those yaller-headed gals in the saloons of Seattle will lift a poor old grizzled prospector's pay-load almost before he's tied up his mule to the hitching-rail."

We made camp for the night in a small canyon not far from a bluff, which is something like a butte only a different colour.   When we had got the fire nicely going to keep away the elks, bears, bobcats, chipmunks, grouse and Chinese ring-necked pheasants, we fell to yarning under the starlit sky, in about three feet of snow.   We were wrapped in a blanket each, and we had made a good meal of beans, sourdough and coyote meat.   As we yarned over our blackened mugs of instant coffee we could hear the cougars snarling in the ponderosa pines and the convertibles pounding along the highway not twenty yards from our heads.   There was a drizzle of rain.

" Well," I drawled, " I guess this sure has got Fifth Avenue licked to a frazzle, what? "

My pardner spat in the fire.   From where he lay he could hit the fire one time out of three.   (As a matter of fact after a few hours he put it out altogether, and we had to move down the road a piece to an hotel.)

" Yes, sir," he replied,   " Ef I had to choose, I'd choose Fifth Avenue every time.   But seeing how I *don't* have to choose, I choose the Wenatchee Mountains, and I reckon I always will."

When we parted next morning he directed me to the Oregon Trail and gave me a letter of introduction to a Paul Bunyan.   I never found the Oregon Trail (it is obliterated during the rainy season), but I finally reached Seattle,

where they told me that this Bunyan chap had just that minute checked out. Seattle was the most hard-boiled spot I'd seen since Westport, Conn., with a law against jay-walking, the highest suicide rate in the country, and the biggest concrete pontoon bridge in the world. (I have been trying to find out where all the *other* concrete pontoon bridges in the world are, but so far without success.)

In the 1860s a person called Asa Mercer, president of the university, put Seattle on its feet by importing a lot of virgins from the east coast to marry the pioneers. The pioneers had simply been hanging around the saloons playing pool and generally getting the place a bad name, so what with one thing and another this was regarded as the sharpest move the president of any university ever made. Marriage quickly caught on, and before long the pioneers all had clean boots and slicked-back hair: some of them even carried the shopping, and the upshot was that by 1889 the whole of Washington was considered fit to join the Union.

Wherever you go in the Northwest there is scenery, conveniently laid out in State Parks with picnic facilities. There are over forty such parks in Washington alone, ranging in size from 24,000 acres to a couple of fields and a litter-basket. These parks have peaks snowcapped, views spectacular, sites camp, lifts ski, fishing mixed, and fat men in shorts and sunglasses who show you where to stand to get the best snaps. On the Columbia River there is a dam (I forget its name) which is the biggest thing anyone has ever made since the world began. They told me that it weighs three times as much as the Great Pyramid of Cheops. It counts as scenery, but is largely used for making electricity. "And how much electricity," asked my guide with a faint sneer, " have they got in Cheops?" "I don't know," I said, "but who weighed that pyramid for you?" (I find it pays to be ready with biting repartee in this country, where everyone is brought up on the Katzenjammer Kids.) In Washington there is a petrified forest, not to mention a copy of Stonehenge which someone has thoughtfully set up on a cliff in a place called Maryhill (pop. 100). On a 7,000-acre ranch near here there is also a museum in which for 30c. I saw Indian artefacts, personal possessions of Queen Marie of Rumania, and a collection of French mannequins. To tell the truth, there is something for practically everyone. As a sign on a shop in Tillamook said, " If we ain't got it, brother, you ain't going to need it."

Oregon is such a lonely place that parts of it haven't even been found yet. I spent a good deal of time here, watching salmon climbing ladders; went for a ride on some logs; met a lot of Basque shepherds; trod on a marmot in Crater Lake National Park; caught two steel-head, four crappie and a halibut; played cricket in Portland, where roses grow on the telegraph poles; and

finally entered Idaho by way of Hell's Canyon. After that I had to stay a week in Sun Valley, resting up after my arduous crossing of the Snake River (Hell's Canyon is 6,600 feet deep on an average, and one of my shoelaces kept breaking). In Sun Valley I basked all day, getting rid of my frost-bite, while all around me glamorous pink-cheeked slips of girls tobogganed to the music of a mammoth orchestra, the mountains echoing their merry peals of laughter. From here, considerably refreshed, I made my way to Boise, the capital. I was intrigued to find that Boise rhymes not with boys but with noisy. I inquired about this, and they told me that when the French trappers (or it might have been the Basque shepherds) first caught sight of the valley they exclaimed, in their excitable way, " *Les bois! Les bois!* " It must have been a touching scene, and I count this among the most fascinating explanations anyone has ever given me about anything. A great disappointment awaited me in Boise: the Idaho State Penitentiary is closed to visitors and tourists between eleven and one.

As I look back I suppose the most memorable part of my stay in the Northwest (not that I want to boast) was my expedition to climb Mount Rainier with a manufacturing chemist from Wisconsin. He was a great admirer of Hemingway. Mount Rainier is tucked away in a Park in Washington, and it rises to a height of 14,408 feet. Nobody told me this. We set out with light hearts and some bars of plain chocolate down a trail that runs beside Huckleberry Creek. The trail led us to a gas station and a museum in Yakima Park, and that's where we should have stayed. Shortly afterwards we lost the trail altogether, and about four days later we were half-way up the Fryingpan Glacier, living on berries and stuff the bears wouldn't eat. The chemist still swore he knew the place like the back of his hand, and he certainly did his best to prove it. We skirted the Ohanapecosh Glacier, fell in the Muddy Fork River, lay down to die in Paradise Valley, waved our shirts at a passing plane, and finally, on hands and knees, reached an isolated Patrol Cabin somewhere on the Wonderland Trail just before the buzzards came down and flew away with us. It had taken us three weeks, and there was still a lot of park we hadn't even touched.

" What we should have done," said the man from Wisconsin as the ambulance drove across Laughingwater Creek to warm beds and safety, " was to take the Carbon River trail to Mystic Lake, make our way up the Wintrop Glacier, and establish a base on Willis Wall. Of course, from there we would have needed ropes and guides and ice-picks. Still and all," he went on to say, " you got to admit we saw some scenic wonders." We became firm buddies during our convalescence, and I invited him to come and climb the South Downs with me some day. He plans to make the crossing by coracle.

Way Down West

THE West holds many surprises. For instance, when I was a boy the fact that Harold Lloyd first saw the light of day in Colorado was accepted in my immediate circle as a matter of common knowledge; but if you had tried to persuade us that the world's biggest Swiss cheese factory was in Wyoming we would have laughed up our sleeves. It has taken me more than forty years to find out how wrong we would have been, for there was this Swiss cheese factory as large as life, with the milkmaids snoring in the bunkhouse and the jerk-line skinners serenading them under the window with home-made guitars, and I was dumbfounded. Thus does travel broaden the mind.

Another surprising thing about the West is that it *isn't* the place the young men went to when the old men cunningly said " Go West, young man " so that they could have all the blondes in Manhattan to themselves and thus give rise to Peter Arno. The place the young men actually went to was California, and we all know what *that* gave rise to. People sitting around in the desert injecting one another with benzedrine and going into comas.

First things first, however; we are not in California yet. The West is quite different. For one thing Gary Cooper was born in Montana, and the Westerners have been saying " Yup " ever since. They also tend to have uranium in their backyards, but not nearly so much as the Blackfeet Indians, who have it under their wigwams and are frequently prepared to let it stay there. Again, Westerners live with their shirt-sleeves rolled up and are less complicated than Easterners. They are not too proud to settle for a sedan instead of a convertible if need be, and they are not afraid to call a maverick a maverick. They walk as though their feet hurt—another Cooper influence. They will shoot you down like a dog one day and invite you round for flapjacks and molasses the next, with hominy grits and blueberry pie on the side. They live mostly in ghost towns, where their grandfathers died without taking off their boots, fighting posses, claim-jumpers, friends, neighbours, train-robbers and the Flathead Indians. So many of them are descended from participants in the Battle of Little Bighorn River that according to my calculations General Custer's gallant little band amounted to just over a division, and I can't see why he didn't drive those Sioux clear up into Saskatchewan.

The West also contains Utah, one of the few states I know that hasn't had a song written about it, presumably because it doesn't even rhyme with pewter. (Come to think of it, though, Ohio doesn't seem to rhyme with anything special, yet there is a splendid song about Ohio, containing the following lines:

Ohio, Ohio,
If I had the money that I owe there,
I would take a train
And go there.)

Utah wasn't much of a place at all until Joseph Smith made up his mind to populate it, but he certainly got things moving. In fact if he hadn't been discouraged Utah might have stretched half-way across to Rhode Island by now, with the tobacco industry on its last legs and the whole course of history at sixes and sevens. As things are, I found Utah to be an orderly, well-run place, with molybdenum diggers digging for molybdenum, farmers growing sugar-beet, and Latter-day Saints drinking cocoa. They also have a lot of dinosaurs. I had seen nothing like them since my visit to Yale, and I was assured that if they weren't the biggest in the world they were the oldest. I am getting sick and tired of all these dinosaurs. I personally believe that they are made in New Jersey, the whole pack of them, like everything else, and shipped out in crates with packets of screws and assembly instructions and a mimeographed line of spiel for official guides, F.O.B. Detroit, and I said so.

" Also," I said, " I am beginning to have my doubts about some of these stalactites and petrified forests and old burial mounds and so on. What with plastics and Scotch tape and everything, you people could run up a whole scenic wonderland practically overnight, and I wouldn't put it past you. Now, with a thing like Westminster Abbey," I said, " it's a different matter. You know where you *are* with Westminster Abbey."

But you can't shake the Latter-day Saints. " When a man is tired of dinosaurs," they said kindly, " he is tired of life."

In Utah I was taken to see some baseball. I believe my hosts expected me to be astounded, but I found that the game was played exactly as in England. True, there was a parade of drum-majorette baton-twirlers in bathing-costumes,

and the military band of the local branch of the Daughters of the Revolution ran about the field playing selections by Victor Herbert at half-time, dressed as horses; but apart from that I noticed very little that seemed at all out of the way, and I soon took for granted the fact that everybody wore racoon coats and threw empty pop-bottles at the referee. It was a very gay scene. The spectators chewed popcorn and waved triangular flags marked with symbols like CBS and WXO2, and the Latter-day Saint on my left kept giving me strawberry milk-shake from a hip-flask. Altogether I felt exactly like Scott Fitzgerald.

The game itself lacked drama. The Midgets scored first with two runs in the second inning. Grimaldi flied out, Murphy walked, Schiaparelli hit a homer into the lower centre field stands, Schuyler doubled along the left field line, Rizotto rolled out to third, and Smith was out on strikes. A very familiar pattern, as you see. After that O'Grogan hit his second home run over the scoreboard into the bleachers, and Mayevsky walked. Zuckermann hit into a double-play and Garcia scored after an infield hit, with two men on third, Murphy still walking, Mayevsky sneaking home, and the second base umpire appealing against the light. It was all fairly routine stuff, but since I felt bound to show some enthusiasm I clapped from time to time, calling out " Bravo! " My hosts were delighted.

Some days later I went to Montana, which is pretty well overrun by Rockies and has earthquakes into the bargain. The Rockies are such good tourist bait that the earthquakes are rather played down in the brochures. Another feature they don't boast about is the presence of Abominable Snowmen, and I can't say I blame them. I met one in a cabin half-way up Mount Cleveland. It was just over five and a half feet tall, with glasses. It had a musquash coat, no tail, and a woollen hat with a bobble. It said its name was O'Hara, and almost before I had set foot in the place it was trying to sell me insurance.

Montana is said to be bigger than Japan. Whether this is an advantage or not is no real concern of mine. As a matter of fact it might also be said to be less noisy than Japan; and I have always understood that dude ranching, which is a major industry in Montana, plays a relatively small part in the economy of Japan. But there, it seems to me, the comparison ends.

I next visited Wyoming, long famous for its little grey homes. You still have the Rockies to contend with in Wyoming, but there are plenty of flat parts if you take the trouble to look for them. I entered the State early one evening, riding side-saddle on a second-hand burro and suitably dressed in an off-white ten-gallon hat, a bandana sweat-rag, suède chaps, a leather-fringed waistcoat, sénsible shoes, dark glasses, a red flannel shirt, revolving spurs, buckskin gloves, snakeskin braces, sharkskin trousers, and an ammunition-belt

containing a sack of Bull Durham, a fifth of Bourbon and some clean socks. The rest of my equipment—blanket, deck of cards, coffee-grinder, billy-can, fishing-tackle, geiger counter, trenching tool, anti-gas ointment, Colt ·45, Cherokee phrase-book, branding-iron, water-bottle, and mouth organ—were lashed to my pack-mule by lariat, and as I toiled at last up the main street of Cheyenne an old deputy sheriff came lurching out of Clancy's Select Bar and Livery Stable and shook me by the hand. '' Doggone,'' he exclaimed with tears in his eyes, '' if it ain't Hoot Gibson! ''

I was to encounter the same kind of friendliness all over the West.

In Wyoming I stayed with a rancher called Red, whose daughter wore a dimity gown and was in love with the foreman. Like most of his fellow-countrymen, Red was a great joiner. Joining had been his hobby ever since he left high school, and he was already a member of the Simpler Spelling Association, the American Society of Whigs, the Benevolent and Protective Order of Elks, the Izaak Walton League of America, the International Concatenated Order of Hoo Hoo, the Save-the-Redwoods League, and the Society for the Perpetuation of Circus Street Parades. '' A guy gets lonesome,'' he explained, '' out here under the stars. This way I feel I *belong*.''

Wyoming is in the whittling belt, and at night Red and I would sit on the tail-board of a chuck wagon, singing cowboy ditties, with a knife and a lump of kindling apiece, while the prong-horned deer prowled among the dogies and the cowhands sat around the camp fire telling humorous stories. He taught me how to tell which way the wind was blowing, and when not to draw to a bobtailed flush, and how to light a fire with buffalo spoor. He was also full of homespun philosophy. '' Women is plumb different from men,'' he would say, '' but they cost as much to feed in the long run.'' '' If I had fifty thousand dollars,'' he would say, '' I wouldn't be sittin' here on this old ranch: I wouldn't be able to afford it.'' When I left Colorado he gave me some salt pork for the journey, and a photograph of a statue of Colonel William F. Cody by Gertrude Vanderbilt Whitney.

I found Colorado thick with gold and rather bumpy. It has more scenery per square inch than any other state, and to see it you have to put your head back and stare up at an angle of eighty degrees. A survey conducted in 1958 showed that out of every hundred persons in America with a pain in the neck, sixty-five had just got back from Colorado. The remainder were 50 per cent Democrats and 50 per cent Republicans. The only scenic wonder I made a point of asking to see was the Colorado Desert, but they said they'd never heard of it. I found later that it was in California all the time. I thought this an unnecessarily confusing arrangement, but felt it best not to say so.

There is much to be seen apart from scenic wonders, however, and I saw it.   Among other things I saw Cripple Creek, where men fought for gold with their bare hands in the days before less exhausting ways of fighting for it had been organized.   In Denver I saw a Greek temple and an equestrian statue of Kit Carson.   In Leadville (alt. 10,188 ft.) I encountered my first bismuth mine.   I saw a face on a bar-room floor in Central City, and in the San Luis Valley I was shown the biggest crop of cauliflowers in the country.   I asked the man in charge what they did about slugs.

" Well, now," he said.   " First of all we ride 'em down, and then we hog-tie 'em.   Then, if the critters ain't got nobody's brand mark on 'em, we have ourselves a barbecue.   Yes, sir, folks come from miles around."

" I see," I said.   " And these cauliflowers.   How do they compare with the cauliflowers in Texas? "

" Texas? " he replied.   " We *import* cauliflowers from Texas.   They're delicacies in these here parts.   Leastways, *they* call 'em cauliflowers.   We call 'em brussels sprouts."

This passion for exaggeration and hyperbole is very prevalent in the U.S., especially in the Western parts.   I often found it hard to appreciate, having been brought up in a country where understatement is considered a more effective form of emphasis.

The cauliflower incident also reminds me that Americans as a general rule like their food big, and preferably tasteless.   To take a simple instance, if they detect the slightest flavour of bread in a loaf they will take it out at once and bury it three hundred yards from the nearest dwelling, and report the baker to the Department of Sanitation.   After a while one gets used to this. I recall that on one occasion I was just starting on my second crisp roll at dinner when my hostess leaned forward and begged me not to eat the table decorations.   They were plaster of Paris, she said, and had been in the family for years. Tomatoes weighing up to a pound and a half each are quite common, and they taste so pure you could use them as baby soap.   As to meat, I spent a whole week in Colorado, and on the day I arrived they served me a steak.   It lasted my entire stay.   Each night when I got back to my hotel I'd have it sent up to my room.   Then I'd sit down and try to hack another five inches off it.   On the last evening, admitting defeat, I wrapped up the remaining three-quarters of a pound in a towel, and hid it in the wardrobe. Then I checked out. When I got to Dallas it was waiting for me, with a note from the management.

" Sir," said the note, " you never finished your chop."

'The Eyes of Texas are upon you'

I DID not spend much time in Oklahoma, partly on principle (it is a dry State) and partly because I arrived on Will Rogers' birthday and the shops were shut.

Oklahoma was at one time considered to be so useless that it was thoughtfully turned into a dumping ground for Indians, who were marched up from the South by the Army and died like flies on the way, thus demonstrating once again the superiority of the white race, who finished the trip as fresh as daisies. Unfortunately, some time later a lot of oil was discovered under the Osage Indian Reservation, and it began to look as though money was going to find its way into the wrong hands. Suitable arrangements were hastily made, however, and I have no doubt that the Indians got some kind of compensation, such as the right to sell home-made shawls to trippers. (As a matter of fact at more than one stage of my journey through the States I heard reckless talk about letting all Indians vote in elections. Naturally I made no comment, but I hope they know what they're doing.)

I hope Rogers and Hammerstein know what they're doing, too, because most of the elephants' eyes I have seen were higher than any corn I encountered in Oklahoma. The scenery consists mainly of medders, each with a bright golden haze, and oil-derricks. In these parts a man is judged not so much by the number of washing-machines he buys for his wife in an average year as by the size of the oil derrick in his back yard. If you are particularly sensitive to the jibes of your neighbours you can buy a lightweight plastic do-it-yourself derrick which can be erected in next to no time. All you need is a screw driver. They come in a pleasing variety of pastel shades, and for an extra fifty dollars they can be fitted with a lifelike gusher. Things have got so bad in Oklahoma City now that you can hardly cross the road for derricks. As for Cadillacs, these are so plentiful that there were times when I kept thinking I was in Kuwait.

From Oklahoma I made my way into the trackless deserts of Nevada. This was hard, wild country, with here and there a cairn marking the last resting place of some unfortunate fellow who got separated from the herd while doing crowd work on location. I saw several shallow depressions made by the flying saucers which land here from time to time, and I saw Reno, where I was approached five minutes after checking in at my hotel by a free-lance Marriage Guidance Counsellor who entreated me to sit down quietly and think the whole thing over before I wrecked two lives.

" My good fellow," I said suavely, " what brings me here is this: I want to see the evening sun go down over the snow-tipped Sierra Nevada."

Within the hour he had spread this all over the town, and I was pointed out for the rest of my visit as the mad Englishman. It seems that there are people who have spent exactly six weeks in Reno without so much as setting eyes on the Sierra Nevada.

Reno is a wide-open town, and I was told that this was due to the silver-mining that goes on in the vicinity. " Where you have miners," they said, " you're *bound* to have gambling and high life. It's an historical fact." " I suppose you're right," I said, recalling the riotous nights I used to spend in the Lancashire coalfields in my youth, eating chipped potatoes until all hours and playing pontoon for matches.

Superficially, Las Vegas is something like Reno, but on closer inspection it proves to be even more like Blackpool during Wakes Week. It is also wider open than Reno, probably because it's closer to the Equator. There are fruit-machines everywhere (I found one in my boot-cupboard) and nothing ever closes, even if the sheriff comes in with a posse and takes away the floor-show in a wagon. If ever a town was an embodiment of the old saw " Americans know how to live," this is it. I spent three whole days and nights smoking king-size cigarettes and shooting craps in an establishment as big as St. Paul's, called the Diamond Studded Dollar, and that's a thing you couldn't do in Runcorn. There was also some kind of a cabaret turn going on—Yehudi Menuhin, or Zsa Zsa Gabor, or someone like that—and every now and again the foundations of the place were shaken by an atomic explosion.

" Don't you ever feel," I asked a croupier, " rather like those people who were dancing on the eve of Waterloo? "

" No," said the croupier, " I feel fine. Only thing is, my feet hurt."

It was shortly after this that I happened to come across Texas—more or less by accident, really, owing to some mix-up about trains.

The truth is, I had thought I might glance at it as we passed through if I happened to be awake, for I had heard it was not without interest, if inclined to be flat. However, finding myself set down on a remote wayside halt in a sort of field, and being assured that this was in fact Texas, I decided to occupy myself with a tour of investigation. There was some time to wait before the next train, and I felt it would be churlish simply to sit in the waiting-room.

Nobody, by the way, could fail to be fascinated by American trains. For one thing, they are the only trains I know which go grinding and clanking through the very hearts of towns, at street level, preceded by a man with a red flag. This gives rise to a peculiarity of American town-planning: on one side of the tracks you will see the well-to-do hanging about waiting for the jewellers' shops to open, while on the other side the poor will be grubbing for scraps in the trash-cans. Then again, the trains always start from some vast echoing temple with a carillon and a misleading name. (In New York they have a station called Pennsylvania, and in Philadelphia they presumably have one called Kansas City, and so it goes on.) You can telephone from a train if you are an accredited executive*, and even if you are not you can take a bath in a train, or post a letter, or play deck tennis in the Lounge Hall, or get married, or enjoy a session of square-dancing in the Rumpus Coach, or order a grey flannel suit. The back of each train is open to the sky, with a railing. These draughty *patios* are for the convenience of passengers who happen to be running for President. They are allowed to have the train stopped at every cross-roads so that they can lean over the rail and promise a handful of innocent bystanders that they're going to introduce piped water and raise the price of hogs.

The sleeping arrangements are sensational, the bunks being placed one above another along each side of the coach, and hidden behind curtains. Nobody is ever quite certain which bunk is which, so that a great part of the night is taken up with people in dressing-gowns lurching up and down the centre aisle, opening and closing curtains until the whole train is in an uproar. To add to the din, the engine-driver sounds his siren on the slightest provocation, and if he hasn't a siren he tolls a bell instead. In the day-coach the travelling salesmen, in their two-tone shoes, are whooping it up with root beer and draw poker, while the box-cars and cattle-trucks are loud with the snores of hoboes, escaped convicts, bums, bank-robbers, thimble-riggers, migratory roustabouts and missing persons, some with prices on their heads. One way and another it's just about as lively as the night boat from Holyhead to Dun Laoghaire.

* Anyone higher than the boy who fills the inkwells is an executive. He has a suite.

The coaches have sunshine roofs. They are pressurized, dustproof, pollen-proof, air-conditioned, sterilized, oblong, mothproof, shrink-resisting, stabilized, rustproof and antiseptic. The staff includes a resident manicurist, first and second-class dentists, peanut vendors, the editor of the Train Newspaper, and a porter who wakes you with a glass of iced water at three in the morning to warn you that your station is less than five hundred miles away.

It was through the helpful enthusiasm of one such minion that I found myself standing on this lonely platform watching the train's rear light disappearing up an *arroyo*.

"Look here," I said angrily to a man with a green eyeshade, who was tapping out messages for Western Union in the ticket-office, "this doesn't look much like San Francisco to me. I thought there was supposed to be a bridge?"

"San Francisco?" said the man with the eyeshade suspiciously. "What's that?"

54

Then, as I simultaneously heard the lowing of distant shorthorns and noticed that the man was tall and lean and wore high heels, the truth dawned on me. This was the Lone Star State, birthplace of Ken Maynard, Ginger Rogers and Dwight D. Eisenhower!

Without much more ado I asked him to keep an eye on my baggage, and stepped outside to look the place over.

Perhaps I can best give you some idea of the extent of Texas if I tell you that it is very considerably smaller than Australia and British Somaliland put together. As things stand at present there is nothing much the Texans can do about this, and I noticed that they are inclined to shy away from the subject in ordinary conversation, muttering defensively about the size of oranges. Roughly speaking, Texas is the strip of land that separates Oklahoma from Mexico. It is chiefly used for pasture, although it produces more helium and mohair than any other State. ("Texas Leads the World in Mohair!" is a familiar cry in the streets of Laredo.) Other products include spinach, pecan nuts, fuller's earth, oil, and shrimps.

The dry-as-dust historical background is as follows. Texas broke away from Mexican rule after the slaughter of Davy Crockett in the Mission San Antonio de Valero. (The Mission San Antonio de Valero being too long a name for anyone to remember, they changed it to the Alamo. Even a child could remember the Alamo.) Texas then blossomed out as an independent nation under its able ruler Sam Houston, who presently, in a fit of depression, suggested that the place should become a Crown Colony of Great Britain. This charming development having been avoided in the nick of time, Texas finally agreed to join the Union on its own terms, one of which was that it should be freely acknowledged and admitted, once and for all, preferably in an amendment to the Constitution, that Texas has the prettiest girls in the world, not to mention the longest dark brown man-made navigable underground collapsible viaduct. Since then Texas and the U.S. have gotten along splendidly.

Texans, quite apart from being tall and lean, turned out to be short and stout, hospitable, stingy to a degree, generous to a fault, even-tempered, cantankerous, doleful, and happy as the day is long. The men wear bootlace neckties on account of the pioneer influence (the pioneers always carried a spare pair), and the women, on account of the Spanish influence, hanker after *haciendas* and turn up at the Saturday afternoon rodeos in *mantillas*. In the south they also drink a good deal of *tequila,* which is a spirit made from the juice of the cactus. It has to be taken with a pinch of salt.

I called on a Texan I had previously met in New York. (We had both been entertained by two gentlemen in a bar on Sixth Avenue, and the Texan had succeeded in buying a brick of solid gold from them at a bargain price— much to my chagrin, for I'd set my heart on it.) He had a typical Texan ranch-house, with a log fire in every room, Chippendale ironing boards, Staffordshire china, a view of the Gulf, monogrammed scatter rugs, a wife like last year's Miss Rheingold and a daughter like next year's. His convertible was brand new, but he had had it impregnated with a special concoction to make it smell of very old leather and spaniels. It was fitted with a shower, a herb garden, a folding boudoir, an ashtray, and an electric device for sharpening scythes, which was new to me, and didn't work.

I suppose Texas is principally famous for the statue of Popeye in Crystal City. It is a momentous work, certainly, but I must say I saw several other things which seemed worthy of mention. In San Antonio, for example, there are poverty-stricken Mexicans of the most picturesque and photogenic nature imaginable, while a little to the south lies a farm called the King Ranch, ruled over by semi-feudal barons and noticeably smaller than metropolitan France.

Texas is certainly a region of superlatives. In the university I saw the largest collection of mystery stories in existence, and in Pecos County I saw the deepest hole. In Jacksonville I was introduced to the ugliest dog in the world, in Dallas I used the bluntest knife, in Austin I slept on the hardest bed, and on Robinson Boulevard, El Paso, I heard the oldest joke. Also, Texans wear far bigger hats than anybody else, and one can't help wondering why.

All the same, Texas is a pretty little place, and I don't care who hears me say it, within reason. I'm glad I was able to fit it in. I shall long remember the sound of mission bells wafting across the *mesas* full of cotton, the million-aires playing pitch and toss for chains of hotels in the cocktail bars of Houston, the pearl-grey Stetsons of the bootblacks in Dallas, the cowhands singing all night long in the streets of Fort Worth, and the stripper in the Amarillo night-spot who has to do her act behind a barbed-wire entanglement on pay-nights. And, just to be on the safe side, I shall remember the Mission San Antonio de Valeras.

Hollywood and Environs

THE first thing that happened when I reached the Californian border was that grim-faced guards hustled me into a hut and turned me upside-down.

I had already assured their people in Grosvenor Square, W.1, that I had no concrete plans for overthrowing the United States government, but that wasn't enough for the Californians: they wanted to know how I was fixed for plant pests.

" Look here," I said recklessly, " I have nothing to declare and I claim the Fifth Amendment." So they pinioned my arms and went through all my pockets, finally laying on the table eight dandelion seeds, an old piece of Formby asparagus, a life-size rubber beetle for dropping in people's beer and making them laugh, and some things they said were ants' eggs. To make matters worse, in the boot of my convertible they found a boll weevil.

" What the hell are you doing with this boll weevil? " they said. " What d'you *think* I'm doing with it," I said, for my keen native sense of fun had not deserted me: " giving it a lift? I demand to see the British Consul! "

" You pipe down," they said, and they ferreted in the turn-ups of my trousers until they found some bits of ground-elder root, a mealy bug, two red spiders and what appeared on the face of it to be a carrot fly. " Good God," they said, " this guy's loaded with the stuff. Lock the door! "

Eventually, after two days, during which time they fumigated my knapsack, sprayed me with D.D.T. and gave me a crew cut, I was taken out of quarantine and allowed to proceed, on the strict understanding that I didn't plant any blackcurrants in the San Joaquin Valley.

I would be one of the last to deny that foreign travel is an agreeable way of passing the time if you've nowhere else to go, but I'm bound to admit that bad luck tends to dog a good many of my footsteps on this trip. I had made a special point of visiting California (it is a long, narrow place down the bottom left-hand side, bravely staring Red China in the face and notable as the world's chief source of syrup of figs and tennis players) for the express purpose of seeing the annual Horned Toad Derby at Coalinga. You can imagine my chagrin, therefore, when I found that this spectacle takes place in May, which meant that I was both three months too late and eight months too early. It was a bitter blow, certainly; but I was greatly consoled when they consented to show me the stadium in which the Derby is actually held, with seats for sixty thousand and standing room for twice that number. I also saw the totalisator buildings, the hot-dog stands, the judge's box, the photo-finish camera, the stables, the paddock, the weighing-in room, and the living accommodation for Horned Toad handlers, vets, owners and breeders. The Horned Toads themselves were scattered far and wide in their various training quarters, undergoing the most rigorous exercise and being injected with vita-mins the livelong day. However, it needed only a slight stretch of the imagina-tion to picture the scene on that thrilling day in May, when Coalinga is loud with the thunder of Horned Toads' feet, and excitement reaches fever pitch as the favourite turns into the home straight, croaking like crazy, with the Members' en-closure awash with Californian champagne and maddened punters throwing sand in the eyes of the outsider as he tries to hop through on the rails. Add to all this the raucous cries of the fortune-tellers and three-card trick concessionaries, the strident music of the calliopes and carousels, and the distant hooting of pleasure yachts in San Francisco Bay, and you will have some idea about what makes California the Mecca of Horned Toad Derby enthusiasts the world over.

Other people go there too, of course, for where else but in Glendale, to take a single example of the marvels that await the conscientious traveller, could you hope to be shown a reproduction of the church where Annie Laurie worshipped (free, 8.30 a.m. to 5.30 p.m.)? Where else but in El Pueblo de Nuestra Señora la Reina de los Angeles, to take another, could you expect to see a citizen being arrested for shooting rabbits from a streetcar?

One thing they lack in California is rain. It happened in Monterey that I fell into conversation with a lady who was leaning out of the window of her converted Mission house to pick a few oranges for supper, and I casually asked her what the mean annual rainfall might be in, say, San Francisco.

" We do not have rainfall," she said, removing the red rose from her mouth and smiling graciously. " We have precipitation: 20·51 inches in San Francisco, if you must know, and 14·54 inches in Los Angeles."

Apart from that it has been claimed that California produces more Nobel Prize winners than Texas. For all I know this may be a notable achievement, but we must set against it the fact that California also contains two hundred acres called Disneyland, in which are incorporated Adventureland, Frontier-land, Fantasyland, and To-morrowland. This valuable piece of real estate lies twenty-two miles south-west of Los Angeles on the Santa Ana Freeway, but it need not disturb your life if you are prepared to make a wide detour. I was prepared, and in this way I managed to see a good deal of the State and find out what makes it tick so loudly.

I went to a place called Carmel, which was established as a retreat for artists and writers in 1904. I don't know what artists and writers wanted to hide from in 1904, and I don't know whether they had to provide their own pencils and paper, but there are still some of them there to-day. They are fed at four o'clock every afternoon. What they are chiefly hiding from now is income tax. I drove along El Camino Real, which is translated as U.S. Highway 101. I saw a church built in the shape of a barrel at Asti. I saw policemen on the beat in San Francisco. They chase burglars up and down perpendicular streets in convertibles with very bouncy suspension, and when the burglars climb on to the rigging of the Golden Gate Bridge and shake their fists, they shoot them through the head from behind packing-cases. The burglars then fall dead into the harbour, and very few trials are necessary. This does not entirely discourage burglary, but it certainly gives the police an edge on their buddies at week-end duck-shoots. I asked about Saroyan in the Sacramento Valley, and the simple peasants said " Ah, yes, life is good and sad and true and fine and funny and cockeyed and there are flowers and children and Chesterfields and Sibelius and there is love and the movement of the planets, and who could ask for more in Sleepy Valley? "

I came across an encampment of members of the " beat " generation, who were then prevalent in California. They seemed to be mostly around forty years old, and were living on remittances from home in a collection of derelict caravans. I passed a pleasant evening with them, drinking methylated spirits for kicks and throwing lumps of earth at passers-by. They spend a good deal of their time reading one another's novels aloud and crying. Before I left I gave them a parcel of cuddly toys, for which they were aggressively grateful. " Nobody understands us," they told me. " But that's not our chief misery. The day's going to come when *everybody* understands us, and it's going to be absolute *hell*." I drove deep into the interior of a Sequoia Redwood tree, where I met an old man who remembered Bret Harte, but not very clearly.

I saw Los Angeles. It is chiefly given over to private eyes. There are more of them to the square inch than in any other city I know. They sit in shabby offices drinking Scotch with their hats on and waiting for loosely-dressed blondes to drift up in cream convertibles to offer them a five thousand-dollar retaining fee. " My husband is a pig and has gone on a business trip to Santa Anita," murmur the loosely-dressed blondes languorously. " Do come to my Spanish-style beach house, where we can be alone. I think someone is going to be murdered." I visited some poets. They were sitting in the desert in deck-chairs, passing round a bottle of mescalin and arranging twigs in vases according to the principles of Zen. Their conversation was fragile, and they spent their evenings patiently reading through their press-cuttings and hoping to attain *satori*.

Throughout the State I found a considerable preoccupation with death and the disposal of cadavers, and I put it down to the climate, which is so monotonously healthy that the morticians have to bribe people into dying by offering them attractive surroundings for their ashes, on deferred terms. Since the natives are apt to be depressingly long-lived, the morticians are now beginning to advertise in newspapers as far away as Minnesota. " Come to California and Die! " they urge. " You'll Never Regret It! " Needless to say, fortunes are being made out of lead-lined caskets and non-spill embalming fluid, and on the wall of my hotel in Pasadena there was a notice which read: " In case of earthquakes or fatal stick-ups during the night, visitors are requested to leave the telephone number of their regular mortician with the desk clerk. Please also deposit five dollars for shaving and laying-out— returnable in the event of survival. We provide the pennies for your eyes. Rest in peace with the compliments of the Management."

In Los Angeles I met a lady of twenty-nine who showed me the box which will contain her earthly remains. She keeps it in her bottom drawer. There is a small compartment for book-matches, and when you lift the lid it plays " Solveig's Song " from the *Peer Gynt Suite*. " It is my favourite number," she said.

It also appears that Californians are very holy. Where an ordinary person might spend a wet Saturday clearing out the lumber room, a Californian is quite likely to sit down with a scratch-pad and draw up the rules of a new religion. The result is that every third man you meet is a sect in himself, and during my short stay I lived through the end of the world twice (first on the Tuesday, and again on the Friday), and played gin rummy with a lady who had just spent forty thousand dollars building a temple where she and her sister-in-law can worship a smooth flat stone which forms the exact centre of the universe.

" We found it quite by chance," she told me, " on a vacant lot."

She said that she and her sister-in-law had the whole religion to themselves at the moment, but they were hoping to persuade her brother, a travelling salesman, to do some proselytizing on a commission basis. " The main plank in our platform is that human beings are a figment of the imagination," she said, " but we aim to add a few other beliefs, to make the prospectus attractive to younger people."

Finally, I gave in and went to Hollywood. Hollywood, of course, had tried to get me for years, because my books all have such pretty jackets. I had resisted stubbornly—partly out of pride, partly on account of the fare. But that was long ago, in the days when Louise Fazenda, Stepin Fetchit, Karl Dane and George K. Arthur were still names to conjure with. What a change has come over Hollywood since then! I stood for an hour at Hollywood and Vine waiting to be offered a screen test, and all that happened was that I was run in on suspicion by the Highway Patrol for being on foot.

Hollywood is well on the way to becoming a ghost town. You can still meet people who remember the era of moving pictures, but all they are really interested in is getting into a thirty-nine week TV situation-comedy series, like everybody else. The stately domes of Beverley Hills are crumbling into dust, and in the Brown Derby I only came across five people who were writing satirical books about the film colony, whereas in the old days they used to sit in serried ranks, each with a bowl in front of him for hush money. I was still able to see the day-and-night procession of grey-haired pilgrims wending their way to the shrine of Rudolph Valentino in Longpre Park, but at Grauman's Chinese Theatre they were having a hard time finding any people willing to stand in wet concrete for the sake of posterity. They even offered *me* twenty dollars for an impression of my left thumb. " You're nuts," I said: " I'm nobody." " So what? " they said. " So at least you got a gimmick."

Owls were nesting in the deserted, cavernous studios, and on every hand I heard rumours that Hedda Hopper will soon have to switch to knitting twin-sets. The private swimming-pools along Sunset Boulevard were overgrown with weeds. Gone were the carefree shouts of photogenic ex-truck-drivers pulling down their ten thousand bucks a week and chasing pneumatic beauty queens through the dim-lit night-clubs. The beaches at Malibu and Santa Monica, empty now of starlets romping for the photographers from girlie magazines, were littered instead with Daiquiri-soaked television moguls thinking up quiz-show questions at the edge of the wide Pacific. And always, wherever I went in this sun-drenched suburb, there were the lynx-eyed men in snap-brimmed hats, lurking behind palm-trees compiling their classified lists of Commies, near-Commies, ex-Commies, fellow travellers and open admirers of Bevan. For the work of keeping Hollywood free from sin has never ceased for an instant since the first un-American was chased out of town for sniggering at Cecil B. de Mille.

Moonshine and History

LIKE Daniel Boone before me, but prudently wearing a different kind of hat, I entered Kentucky by way of the Cumberland Gap and made my way first to the famous cliff-dwellings of the mountain men. They are hard to find. Wild beasts abound, and such paths as exist are precipitous. Now and then I came across a sign, something on these lines:

THIS WAY TO THE MOUNTEN MEN

Travelers pass this point at their *own risk*.

Bewar stray arows.

Engage botom gear.

DO NOT feed the natives.

It is certainly an eerie region. The air is loud with the rattle and squeak of home-made banjos, mouth-organs and fiddles, for the mountain men crouch all day in their ramshackle cabins on the look-out for the folk-music collectors who swarm about the craggy wastes with tape-recorders hoping to pick up some early nineteenth century skiffle number for a few bangles or a bar of soap and flood the market with it. Since the mountain men use a good deal of soap for roasting their opossums, they are always ready to ad lib a four-in-a-bar master-piece at the drop of a hat. If in the fullness of time it sparks off a rock-'n'-roll riot in Hamburg or Tokyo they receive the news with a grunt and the ejection of a mouthful of Burley juice. (This in fact is how they have *always* received news. Almost every day another little colony gets word that the Declaration of Independence has finally been signed, and the most excitement they ever show is to go out and shoot a cousin, or ''neighbour'' as they call them.)

They are hairy people with hardly any privies, descended from good Anglo-Saxon stock and slightly less socially acceptable, by Lexington standards, than the pygmies of the Congo. They never clean their shoes, and they usually

sleep with a loaded blunderbuss handy.   The women are distinguishable from the men by the fact that they take their pipes out of their mouths to spit.   They don't like people much.   They have always strenuously avoided being included in any census, and nobody knows quite from one day to another just how many of them there are.   (I counted nine hundred with clothes, and forty-three without.)   Blood-curdling tales are told of explorers who have penetrated into their trackless wilderness bent on sociological research or an investigation into the possibility of selling them washing-machines, and have never returned.

" One half of them we et," I was told by a man called Zeke, who seemed to be some kind of chief, " and one half of them was too stringy so we made them into witch-doctors.   That'll larn the critters not to come a-sneakin' and a-spyin' in these here parts, I reckon."

" But, goldarn it," I said, " what about their families? "

" Ef it's kin they want," said Zeke, " there's plenty hereabouts and to spare."

I asked Zeke how he passed his time, and he told me that in the winter he mostly sleeps, in the spring he chases some likely female cousin about the rocks, in the summer he makes moonshine whisky out of potato peelings and coffee grounds, and in the fall he mostly drinks it.

" I kin shoot a bar," he said, " at fifty paces, ef so be it don't a-see me fust.   I use nails and trouser-buttons as ammunition.   I had me a bath but once in my life, and danged if it didn't shrink my underpants so now they don't hardly reach my ankles."

He is a hundred and three.   The only thing he ever reads is a copy of the *Louisville Courier-Journal* which blew into his shack during a big storm in 1911. He aims to get through to the sports section before he dies.   His main fear is that the railroad may eventually push its way as far south as Kentucky and scare away the jack-rabbits; for, as he says, he ain't a-figgering to start making stew out of anything else at his time of life.   " I tried snakes," he told me, " but a snake's bones aren't hardly worth chewing."   (He has teeth.   He got them by mail order, and keeps them in an old bean-can under the bed.)

These mountain men are strictly preserved, like the lions in Kenya.   It is interesting to note that those who can be persuaded to vote at all will almost invariably plump for the Republican candidate.   I brought back with me a representative collection of their stone implements, and a photograph of a typical chief drinking with his wives at a water-hole.

I would have liked to stay longer, but after a couple of weeks, besmirched with the smoke from kerosene lamps and filled with a great longing to eat food with a knife and fork, or at least a spoon, instead of a dipper made from the lid of a tobacco-tin, I bade farewell to the mountain folk and lowered myself down towards civilization, dodging as best I could the jagged rocks, frying-pans, dead dogs, bedsteads and home-made hatchets they hurled after me.

" Come agin, neighbour! " they called, their voices echoing and re-echoing among the hills. " Bring a friend! "

As you may imagine, the rest of Kentucky proved to be something of an anti-climax. Down in the plains I found that the inhabitants had achieved a relatively high degree of culture, and produce things like hay, turkeys, bituminous coal, bourbon and clay. The capital of the State is Frankfort, and the dome of the State Capitol is an exact reproduction of Napoleon's tomb.*

Most of America's famous people were Kentuckians, a notable exception being Shirley Temple. Carrie Nation lived in Lancaster, the birth of D. W. Griffith took place in Le Grange; and Alice Higgins Rice first saw the light of day in Shelbyville—insisting when she grew up, against the advice of several of her friends, on writing *Mrs. Wiggs of the Cabbage Patch*. Abraham Lincoln was born in Kentucky, and to complicate matters so was Jefferson Davis. This seems to have given rise to some considerable confusion, for I was told that during the War between the States (known elsewhere as the Civil War and officially referred to as the War of the Rebellion) Kentucky somehow had ninety thousand men on the side of the Union and forty thousand on the side of the Confederacy. Small wonder that the bitter struggle dragged on.

There are still a good many colonels about, as it happens. I met several, sitting on the porches of their pillared mansions in undress uniform, drinking whisky with mint sauce in it and watching their horses eat blue grass among the magnolia trees. Horses are rather important hereabouts. On one of the horse farms I saw a $50,000 statue of Fair Play, the sire of Man-o'-War; and I need hardly remind you that Man-o'-War himself passed away in 1947, mourned by the whole State. The C. V. Whitney Farm, home of Mahmoud, was on view between the hours of 9 and 4, but in Versailles (rhymes with " gaols ") I was told that if I wanted to see the skeleton of Lexington I would have to go to the National Museum in Washington, D.C. " Great heaven! " I cried, momentarily fogetting my manners as a visiting foreigner. " D'you mean to tell me you don't even have an exact *reproduction* of it here? "

I was impressed by the fact that a monk in a Kentucky Trappist monastery has written several best-sellers, and absolutely delighted to learn that my Old Kentucky Home is preserved as a State shrine; but when I got to Fort Knox

* I have no idea why. When I asked, I was told that America is a free country.

and they refused to let me look around the U.S. Gold Repository, even though I offered them 50c., I'm afraid I lost my temper.

" It's closed to the public," they said.

" Now look here," I said, " I'm a British citizen, and I demand to see where all my money went. You've melted it down into bars," I said, " *and now I want to see it!* "

" Beat it, sonny," they said. " We wouldn't even let the President in here without a chit."

" This is an outrage! " I said. " I have just seen the stalactites at Park City for 78c., plus tax, with a guide thrown in, and yesterday I saw the insect collection in the Baker-Hunt Foundation Museum at Covington *for nothing*. On Thursday afternoon I had a Scenic Boat Trip on the Green River in Mammoth Cave National Park for $1.10. What is more," I said, " I could have taken my pets along with me if they'd been on leash, crated, or otherwise physically restricted at all times. Now stand aside and let me see my money."

" The guy's crazy," they said.

" I see what it is," I said. " You can't fool me. It's all a fake—a monstrous façade to bamboozle the backward nations of the world. *You haven't any gold in there at all!* You've frittered it all away, that's the top and bottom of it! You've squandered it in dribs and drabs, on drink and drugs, and airline tickets for the Secretary of State and rockets to the moon, and all you've got in there now is a lot of old cigar boxes that wouldn't fool a child in the second grade! No, gentlemen, on second thoughts nothing would induce me to set foot in the place, and I bid you a very good day! "

With that they put up their carbines and I went to Virginia.

Apart from tobacco auctions and its plucky refusal to abolish the chain-gang, Virginia is chiefly noted for history. All United States history took place in Virginia*, so that as I drove through the State in a coach-and-pair with a lady called Mary Lou who pointed out places of interest with her parasol, I was able to piece together the whole story of this great nation. It goes like this:

After Raleigh had discovered Red Indians in Virginia, including one called Pocahontas who finished up in Gravesend, a lot of English came to Jamestown to take part in the massacres of 1622 and 1644. With typical British foresight they brought African slaves with them in case they should ever feel the need for railway porters or amusing chaps to sing the blues. This gave rise to

---

* An exception was the Dempsey-Carpentier fight on July 2, 1921, which Dempsey won by a knock-out in the fourth. Owing to some quirk of Fate this occurred in Jersey City, but I'm bound to say that most Virginians will admit that it counts as history, if you get them alone.

the Negro Question, although many people in London's West End clubs to this very day are inclined to give all the credit to Governor Faubus (not a Virginian).   The English colonists presently became obstreperous and refused to pay taxes to the King (not a Virginian either), saying " If this be treason, then make the most of it."   Jefferson (a Virginian) having written a Declaration of Independence and Benedict Arnold (not a Virginian, and very likely a Russian) having burned down Richmond, Virginia framed the United States Constitution, and proceeded to supply most of the Presidents from George Washington right through to Wilson, including Madison, Monroe and Zachary Taylor.   In 1861, as soon as Dan Emmett had composed " Dixie," Virginia decided to secede, and Robert E. Lee (a Virginian) became commander of the Confederate Army of Northern Virginia.   There followed the Civil War, fought entirely in Virginia although sparked off by John Brown (a Connecticut man) being hanged for thinking he could free the slaves by seizing an arsenal at Harper's Ferry (W. Va.).   The war consisted of the first Battle of Bull Run, the second Battle of Bull Run, the battles of Fredericksburg, Spotsylvania Courthouse, Cold Harbor, Cedar Mountain, Brandy Station, Dinwiddie Courthouse, Five Forks, Frayser's Farm, Malvern Hill and the Wilderness.   If you add to these the sieges of Petersburg and Yorktown you will see that presently Virginia began to look very untidy.

During the winter of 1862-63 the opposing armies glared at one another across the Rappahannock River.   When they couldn't stand it any longer they fought the Battle of Chancellorsville, and almost before they'd got properly started Stonewall Jackson (a Virginian) was fatally wounded by gunfire from his own men.   You might think an incident of that sort might pass unnoticed in a Civil War, but it so upset Lee that he surrendered to a fellow called Grant from Massachusetts at the Appomattox Courthouse.   After that it only remained for John Wilkes Booth (not a Virginian) to be shot while resisting arrest at Port Royal, Va., and Virginia was able at last to settle down to the serious business of making Camels and Luckies for those who were left to tell the tale.   That was really the end of American history, if I understood Mary Lou correctly.   The first condensed milk plant was started in 1856, F. W. Woolworth opened a five-and-ten-cent store in 1879, Geronimo surrendered in 1886, the Marines landed in Mexico in 1914, John T. Scopes was fined $100 for teaching Evolution in a high school in 1925, and the F.B.I. shot Dillinger dead outside a cinema in 1934, but all these were simply signs of the times, and did not count as history.   Besides, not a single one of them happened in Virginia.

Indian Territory

O
N my way to the D. H. Lawrence country I stayed for a few nights
in a motel. I cannot be certain that the establishment I chose was
typical, but as it emerged from the dusty desert background, with a
single perpendicular neon sign winking " REST-A-WILE " in two colours, and
a lean, ochre dog slinking up and down the alleys between the two rows of
darkened huts, I was put in mind of a holiday camp suddenly deserted by a
mass evacuation some foggy evening long ago on account of a mysterious plague,
and left to the winds and the slow choking progress of the nettles.

Nothing stirred in this sinister oasis, and yet as I entered the manager's
office I knew that he, and many a silent inmate, had watched my approach
through chinks in the weather-board, and had sized me up as a two-timing
cardsharper from one of the smaller cattle towns, anxious to lie low until the
members of the posse had perished from exposure one by one out there
in the waste lands of the high sierras. He was sly and unshaven, drinking rum
and water from a cardboard cup. His hut was cobwebbed, lit only by moonshine that leaked through a broken window.

" O.K., friend," he said in a croaky voice, when he had assured himself
that my luggage contained no counterfeit bills or kidnapped heiresses, " you're
in Number 8, Block B, Section 2a. Payment in advance and no questions
asked. All I beg of you is that you don't bore no holes through the walls or
leave any evidence. Cook on your gas-ring if you must, but nothing elaborate.
Keep your door locked at all times. And remember, friend, I ain't responsible for nothing."

It was an awesome experience, because it was perfectly clear to me that the
place must be a resort of hijackers, libertines, organizers of unlicensed orgies,
dog-snatchers, passport-fakers, runaway couples and misunderstood husbands

on the loose. How else could one explain the unnatural quiet which cloaked the whole area from morning to night? How else account for the averted eyes, the hastily turned-down hat brim or turned-up collar, the slippered feet shuffling secretly past in the dark, the heavy, guilty breathing in the cupboards, the lighted hut abruptly plunged into darkness as one passed? Why else should small squads of men in long overcoats arrive in the early hours of the morning and tramp about looking for people, their pockets unmistakably filled with loose cartridges? Why else would scribbled messages be pushed under my door by mistake, urging me to meet Lou or Foxy near the gas station at sun-up with the stuff? Nobody can persuade me that all those bursts of satanic laughter after midnight betokened innocent fun, or that there was nothing unseemly about the way a fat, tear-stained woman with yellow hair forced her way twice into my hut wearing a flowered wrapper and called me Gregory. And I never did get the truth about the light which kept flashing " It's me, honey " in Morse from behind a nearby clump of trees on the evening of my arrival.

Encountered separately, all these things might conceivably have seemed trivial enough: taken together, and in conjunction with the cluster of motor-bikes which revved and snarled outside my window all night long, bestridden by scowling lads with knives strapped to their wrists, they were enough to make me decide to sleep beneath the stars in future, out among the mesquite, where the cougar prowls and lonely men are glad to share their beans with passing strangers, dreaming together of their boyhood days before the wander-lust got them.

One night of that, however, was quite enough to make me change my mind: not only was I bitten by innumerable flies, but a chartered accountant trod on my face, returning from a supper-party with his mother and a friend of the family in a georgette frock. From that moment I determined to take the call of the wild for granted and to rely either on proverbial hospitality or third-floor hotel rooms well away from the elevator; and thus I came at last to the region that so captivated Lawrence.

It is certainly an interesting part of the world, and we may be sure that Lawrence was quick to notice many points of difference between New Mexico and his native Nottinghamshire. For one thing, New Mexico is not nearly so cluttered. In the entire State, which covers 121,666 square miles, there are less than three times as many people as there are in the city and county borough of Nottingham. What is more, a good many of them seem to be Spaniards.

SCALPS
65¢
ALL COLORS

LAST CHANCE
BEAD EMPORIUM

PARKING

Historically, too, there are contrasts. Byron lived in Nottingham (or Snotengaham, as the Anglo-Saxons preferred to call it), and it was occupied by William the Conqueror in 1086. The spinning jenny and the stocking frame were both invented in Nottinghamshire, and mammoths are understood to have lived there, not to mention Robin Hood. With New Mexico, however, it is another story. I was told that the place was infested with Stone Age people as far back as the end of the last glacial period (I didn't catch the actual date), while at Taos I myself saw Pueblo Indians of Roman Catholic persuasion sitting outside cliff dwellings built about A.D. 900, with blankets over their heads. In the northwest corner of the State I saw ruins left by the Aztecs, as impressive as any you could hope to find anywhere, and at Lincoln, on the Rio Hondo, the old courthouse is still standing from which Billy the Kid made his famous escape in 1881. As a matter of fact it is a State monument, for he was a most notorious double-dyed brigand, thief and desperado, and his grave at Fort Sumner is as great a tourist attraction as the bats and helictites in the Carlsbad Caverns National Park.

New Mexico is certainly steeped in history and tradition. Kit Carson himself is buried at Taos, and at Shakespeare you can still see the café in which Russian Bill was hanged in 1881. Albuquerque, the largest city in the State, was founded in 1706 and named after the Duke of Albuquerque. Truth or Consequences (pop. 4,563) was named after a radio programme in 1950. At Moriarty, forty-seven miles east of Albuquerque, I visited the Longhorn Ranch Museum and Ghost Town of the Old West, where I saw a Wells Fargo Express Office, longhorn steers, a livery stable, some nickelodeons, and Diamond Jim Brady's 22-carat gold china service. I had to pay 50 cents to get in, but for an extra quarter I could have had a ride in a stage coach.

Probably the most historic region of all, though, is around Alamogordo. Here, as well as pictographs approximately eight hundred years old, I was able to see the exact spot where the first man-made atomic explosion took place on July 16, 1945. It left a sloping crater called Trinity Site, and the Chamber of Commerce conducts regular Guided Caravan

Tours out there free of charge, visitors being expected to furnish their own convertibles. People come from all over the world, to stand around and nudge one another, in brightly coloured shirts, saying " It certainly makes you think " in many languages. They make a gay picture.

Wherever you go in New Mexico you are liable to encounter Indians, and I can assure you that provided you keep your head this need not cause you a moment's alarm: whether they be Apache, Navajo or Pueblo my advice is that you should meet them boldly and stand up for your rights, because the prices of bracelets, baskets, coffee-spoons, cuff-links, blankets, pottery and bedside rugs are more or less standardized throughout the State, and well they know it. To my way of thinking, a good many of these Indians do not look as though they get nearly enough to eat, and I have more than a suspicion that some of their hogans leak. I was not able to ascertain what is being done about this, but I have no doubt that the United Nations Organization has the matter in hand in accordance with its avowed determintaion to reaffirm faith in the dignity and worth of the human person. In the meantime, of course, the Indians are perfectly at liberty to strike oil, or join the Army.

The climate is so wonderful that a good many of the white inhabitants are people who originally came for the good of their health. You can ski here in the morning and stroll through a million-acre sheep-ranch in the afternoon. You can travel for a week by pinto, buying your meagre supplies at Indian trading posts and never hearing a word of English spoken. You can eat sorghum and broomcorn. You can see mesas. You can visit the Teddy Roosevelt Rough Riders' and Cowboys' Reunion on the first Friday, Saturday and Sunday in August, at a little place called Las Vegas. For my own part, I didn't have time to do any of those things, and I'm not going to have the effrontery to pretend that I did, because this is a simple, unvarnished record. I will be candid where it can't be avoided, but I will not attempt to pull the wool over your eyes, and I am not afraid to say that I spent most of my time at a place called Raton, where they manufacture wrought-iron furniture. It was quite a change.

True, I did make a point of visiting Bottomless Lake State Park, which consists of a chain of five lakes so bottomless that one is 190 feet deep; and I did call in at the beautiful city of Santa Fé, if only because it was in the Palace of the Governors there that a former governor of the State called Lew Wallace wrote *Ben Hur*. I noticed something else, too. Santa Fé has a Scottish Rite Temple which is in part a replica of the Alhambra at Granada, and I'll bet *that* isn't a thing they like to be reminded of back home in Nottingham.

From New Mexico, on a sudden impulse, I journeyed into Arizona with neither map nor compass, and before I knew where I was I was panting for water in the Painted Desert, surrounded by organ-pipe cactus, mesquite, creosote, Gila monsters, sagebrush, salt bush and the gaunt ruins of disused tungsten mines. Buttes and plateaux filled the far horizon. Arroyos and canyons crept and threatened me on every side. The colours dazzled my eyes. I could find no wood to build a fire to boil a kettle to make a cup of tea. The sun beat down mercilessly. The crêpe sole on one of my shoes melted clean away. I crawled painfully, inch by inch, into the depths of the Petrified Forest, and as I lay down and closed my swollen eyes my whole past flashed by in a second, with a supporting cast that included thirty-five characters from Zane Grey and the woman in the travel bureau in South Kensington. Just before I lost consciousness I remember thinking " What an extraordinary place to drown! " Two hours later I awoke, to find that I was being carried to the nearest dude ranch by a party of Boy Scouts, slung on a pole like a missionary.

"Brave lads!" I cried. "You shall not go unrewarded for this day's work!"

"Are you kidding? " said the Patrol Leader.

It was not an encouraging start to my sojourn in the Baby State, but I later found much to enjoy. Arizona is noted for copper, winter sports and lettuces, and one out of every twelve people in the State is an Indian. I camped for a week-end in the White Mountains with a party of hunters, and between us we bagged four deer, a wild turkey, a lion and somebody's horse. There are no camels.* I then went to Tombstone, hoping to see the O.K. Corral and possibly an exact replica of Wyatt Earp's moustache. I must say I was rather annoyed to find that the place is now a health resort, and the thing that everyone was most anxious to point out to me was the biggest rose tree in the world, with a trunk measuring fifty-four inches in circumference.

" Doggone! " I said. " If this is Tombstone you can keep it. Danged if I ain't a-fixin' to go to Old Tucson instead! "

I went to Old Tucson. It is on the Tucson Mountain Park Road, and is built mainly of adobe bricks. It was perfect. There was an old mission church (with a graveyard), a jail, a trading-post, a honky-tonk, a stage depot, a saloon, an hotel and a morgue. It was, in fact, the West, and my trigger-finger itched as I walked down the main street and leaned on a hitching-rail with my eyes like slits.

It was put together, brick by brick, by Columbia Pictures in 1940.

* There used to be. They were introduced in 1856, but the going proved too hard for them, and nothing came of it. An Arab called Hadji Ali was imported with them, and I saw his memorial at Quartzsite. It is called the Hi Jolly Memorial. This is all I was able to find out about camels in Arizona.

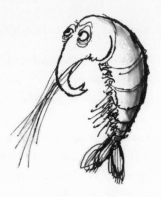

Dear Old Southland

THEY were pulling my leg in Virginia.* The Civil War was *not* fought entirely in that State, and I saw cannon in Georgia to prove it, not to mention some genuine, guaranteed Confederate trenches in Battlefield Park, Jackson, Miss., a jagged hole torn by General Sherman's bombardment at the base of a lamp-post in Atlanta, and the hulks of three Federal gunboats sunk in the Yazoo River and still visible at low water. (One of the cannon was double-barrelled, and four separate people told me that it was the only double-barrelled cannon in the whole, etc., etc. I'm not surprised it didn't catch on: it looked cumbersome to me. That was in a place called Athens, Ga., where they make fertilizer.) Besides, if the whole war took place in Virginia, one might be inclined to ask what all those people were doing marching through Georgia, hurrah, hurrah.

The fact is that Georgia is very old, and has nearly as much history behind it as Virginia, or even Northumberland. There are people living in Georgia to-day who could trace their ancestry back to the Mound Builders, if they would only stir themselves and start making some inquiries. These Mound Builders built mounds in Georgia in prehistoric times, because it was all they were good at. (Some of their music is still on record, played by the Mound City Blue Blowers.) After a while they went away and were succeeded by the Creek and Cherokee Indians, who lazed about half naked, smoking, until the English sent out a man called Oglethorpe to start a colony and see if there was anything worth lifting. "Oh God," said the Creeks and Cherokees resignedly, knocking out their pipes, "here comes the British." So General Oglethorpe was appointed military commander-in-chief, Wesley came out

* If it comes to that, I have my doubts about one or two things they told me in New York, now that I look back on them. For example, there must surely have been something fishy about the claim that New York is the only city in the world which exports baseball teams?

hot-foot to preach, and everything went from bad to worse in typical historical fashion, until people as far away as Boston, Mass., were emptying tea into the Atlantic and supplementary questions were being asked in the House.

George Washington spent a good deal of his time during the ensuing *fracas* being entertained in stately *ante bellum* mansions all over Georgia, and so did Lafayette, a curly-headed French lad who came out to seek a bubble reputation and be like a son to Washington. Washington kept on throwing his arms around him, a style of soldierly behaviour which does not seem to have much impressed General Patton during his formative years—possibly because it is no longer included in the curriculum at West Point.

After the British had been cleared out there was a period of calm, during which the good people of Georgia devoted themselves to the task of perfecting their southern accents so that there would be no misunderstandings when the Civil War started. In due course General Sherman arrived, breathing fire and slaughter, and I was assured that they will not forget him in a hurry in these parts: quite apart from the incident with the lamp-post, he burned Atlanta to the ground without so much as a by-your-leave before setting out on his epic march to the sea—and in the course of that he went out of his way to make a shambles of every town of any note in the State. (Sherman's drive to the sea, incidentally, was launched from Chattanooga, Tenn., and while I was there I naturally paid a visit to Union Station, knowing that Chattanooga is famous for its rolling stock. You may imagine my surprise when I found that they still have an old wood-burning locomotive there called The General, which played a significant part in delaying Sherman's Georgia campaign. It was captured by Union raiders near Atlanta, you may remember, and recaptured by Buster Keaton in the penultimate reel. It looks as good as new.)

By the time the nation's domestic differences had been resolved, four-fifths of Georgia's wealth had vanished, and the Northern army of occupation soon polished off the remainder. One way and another, I was not at all surprised to find, chalked on a wall in a Colonial-style vacant lot in Jonesboro, Ga., the dreaded inscription: YANKS GO HOME!

Still, you can't keep these Southerners down. They may not say much, and what they do say they're inclined to say slowly, but they get things done, and it wasn't long before Georgia was back on its feet again. The lack of slaves hampered them at first, but once they had got used to the idea of shelling their own peas they soon began to prosper. And in 1886, when somebody in Atlanta finally managed to uncover the secret (long hidden from mankind) of how to make Coca-Cola, thus ushering in a new era and a way of life that has

triumphantly survived two world wars and the development of the sliced loaf, things really started to move. Georgia to-day is a thriving State, and as I drove across it, the wheels of my convertible squelching deliciously through the peaches that keep falling from the trees in sackfuls, I was enthralled by the cleanness of the air, the grace and politeness of the people, and the swimming-pool in the Franklin D. Roosevelt State Park, which is made in the shape of the Liberty Bell. Georgia is also noted for peanuts, tobacco, sewer pipes and chenille bedspreads. The maximum speed permitted is 60 m.p.h. (50 m.p.h. after dark). The State motto is "Wisdom, Justice, Moderation," and up to five years ago they had had five hundred and thirty lynchings (a national record).

As a wide-eyed foreigner, and a sentimental one to boot, I suppose the things that most impressed me in Georgia were Tobacco Road, which is rather bumpy and runs south from Augusta, lined by poor-whites living in cardboard boxes; Eatonton, where the creator of Br'er Rabbit was born; and the Okefenokee Swamp, where the Swannee River rises, thinly disguised as the Suwannee. Way down upon it I heard the sound of voices harmonizing Methodist hymns—the humble cotton-workers relaxing in their shanties during a coffee-break. In one typical shanty, where eleven American citizens of African extraction lived cheek by jowl without so much as a chenille bedspread between them, I was rewarded by a gale of heart-warming, full-throated laughter when I asked if they were content with their lot. Such people are to be found in great numbers in the South, and despite the tedious provisions of the Constitution of the United States of America, many of them have been graciously relieved of the necessity of voting at elections—or even, in some cases, of going to school.

Much of the folk-lore of the United States consists of songs written as though to be sung by Americans of African descent, with banjo accompaniment. These songs express an urgent desire on the part of the singer to return to a cabin, a mother, a sweetheart, or an agricultural scene in such areas as Georgia, Alabama, or Mississippi. Why they should wish to revisit these districts is something of a mystery, for in this region Americans of African descent are regarded by many of their paler fellow-countrymen (who stem mostly from English stock) as only barely qualifying for inclusion in the human race as at present constituted.

Although fully aware that this was none of my business, I felt that since I live in a country with a small but growing population of non-Europeans, it might not be amiss if I were to try to learn something about the kind of problems we may have to face ourselves. One evening on the Mississippi Delta, therefore, in a stately *ante bellum* mansion, I asked a kindly old gentleman to explain the whole situation to me.

We were at dinner.   All was candle-light and graciousness, white moustachios and exquisite phials of smelling-salts.   The ladies were elegantly gowned and carried fans, behind which they ogled the handsome sons of plantation-owners across the gleaming napery.   Magnolias and azaleas tapped the window panes.   From the woods outside I could hear the mocking-birds singing, as they must have sung on that fateful night in 1863 when Grant secretly moved up the Union forces for the siege of Vicksburg.   The panelled dining-room was fragrant with the smell of freshly sliced watermelon, and round the walls there hung sabres, flags, and portraits of Confederate generals in uniform.   A silver-haired serving-man in a simple livery kept our glasses charged with French wines and native whiskies—for although the South is inflexibly dry, a stronghold both of the Women's Christian Temperance Union and of the Anti-Saloon League, it remains one of the hardest-tippling regions in the country, with an alarming rate of drunkenness and crime.

No sooner had I broached the question, than a silence fell over the assembled company.   Strong white teeth clamped on black cheroots.   Here and there a fan fluttered more violently, to cool a suddenly overheated cheek; and I realised I had overstepped the line that divides good breeding from the behaviour of a cur.

It was not until the ladies had withdrawn, and the serving-man had shuffled away without any expression on his dark, polished face, that my host vouchsafed any reply to my enquiry.   He explained the situation in solemn, measured terms, and the other guests signified their approval of each point as he made it, by grinding out their cheroots in the crystal ashtrays, or nodding gravely over their jewelled snuff-boxes, or stroking the ornately decorated handles of their six-shooters.   And so, gradually, the scales fell from my eyes.

The situation, I learned, was simple, clear-cut, and deadly.   It amounted to nothing less than the urgent necessity for preserving the supremacy of the white race in the United States.   Already nearly half the population of Mississippi was Negro, and unless strong measures were taken, such as forcing them to worship the Christian God in separate non-white chapels clearly marked to avoid any misunderstanding, it would not be long before they spread like some deadly blight throughout the entire country, taking over the reins of government, making money, disbanding the Klan, and finally driving the white race clean into the sea, chanting their bloodthirsty lays as their medicine-men urged them on to fearful pillage and slaughter.

The candles were burning low in the silver candlesticks.   Whenever the old man paused, leaning back in his chair to straighten his cravat while he

composed a telling phrase, the silence would be broken only by the sound of bourbon splashing musically into a goblet, or the ticking of the Colonial-style grandfather clock that stood in a shadowy corner of the room. Darkness crept up and deepened at the windows; there was a sighing of wind in the live oaks and cypresses; frogs croaked a sinister chorus far off in the swampland; steamboats hooted sadly on the Mississippi River. The blackness outside seemed to be pinpointed with lights from a million hostile eyes, moving ever stealthily closer, crowding in upon this last pathetic stronghold of a crumbling white man's world. I could not but admire the gallantry of these Southern gentlemen, who insist on living their traditionally gracious lives as though quite unaware of the peril that confronts them.

Clearly, I thought, it is wrong for outsiders to criticise the regional or tribal customs of a foreign land, without first taking some pains to *understand* them. I count myself fortunate to have had an opportunity to learn at first hand the bloodcurdling truth of the matter. On my return to New York, indeed, I took care to warn as many of the inhabitants as possible of their imminent danger. " And what is more," I told them, " unless you have *visited* the South, and heard the truth from the lips of those brave men and women who even now are standing firm and steadfast in the front line for your sakes, you must not presume to judge the rights and wrongs of the matter. Ignorance and prejudice," I said, " cannot be used as a basis for civilised argument."

I think I shook them up a little, although their complacency is so deep-rooted that I have actually seen them playing baseball with descendants of men who were chained together and used as slaves by the English colonists.

But there was something I did not tell them: something so terrible that I could not bear to see their stricken faces as they heard it. It was told to me by that same old Southern gentleman as we strolled in the open air on that sultry evening after dinner, the tips of our cheroots glowing in the velvet Mississippi dark. He explained that he had hesitated to mention this final point while we were still at table, for like a good host he had wished to spare me any embarrassment. I must ask you to imagine the horror which descended on me as, by degrees, he whispered his final, shattering revelation. The Negroes, it seems, have an even more dastardly ambition—an ambition so unspeakable that the good old man could not put it into actual words, even out there under the warm cloak of the darkness. But he left me in no doubt about what it was: the very questions he put to me, concluding with one crowning, devastating question, showed me in a blinding flash of comprehension the depths of their abandoned infamy.

They want to marry my sister.

I next visited Louisiana, a very romantic State, where they grow a lot of tung nuts. (I'm afraid I can tell you very little about the tung nut, beyond the fact that it contains more tung per square inch than any other kind of nut; and, as a man in Baton Rouge told me, if it's tung you're after, you'd be a fool to plant anything else. As to tung itself, I see I have a note in my diary, " Pursue inquiries *re* nature of tung, with particular ref. to shape, specific grvty., viscosity and resistance to rust," but all I can find in my notebook under *Tung* is the telephone number of a shrimp millionaire's widow I met at a masked ball during the Mardi Gras. She was to make two reservations for Honolulu without fail the very next afternoon so that we could get away from it all, and I never found out any more about her, either.)

Louisiana was claimed for France, in what seems to have been a rather high-handed fashion, by a man called La Salle in 1682. This gave the place a naughty reputation from the word go, and when they established the city of Nouvelle Orleans in 1712 the shape of the future was plain to see: kissing in public, coffee-bars, the dancing of cotillions, strip joints on Bourbon Street, and Voodoo rites in Beauregard Square. Fearing something even worse, such as the eventual birth of the blues, France dropped the territory like a hot potato in 1762 and gave it to the Spaniards, who were delighted. Nobody was surprised that the first Governor sent out by Spain was a man called General O'Reilly, for even in those days practically everyone's mother tended to hail from County Mayo. Three years later, to add a further cosmopolitan touch to the place, some Acadians settled in the Bayou Teche area, having been chased out of Nova Scotia, where they were mistaken for Arcadians and suspected of being on the point of inventing the musical comedy. In order to disguise themselves they changed their name to Cajuns. They didn't fool O'Reilly, but the name stuck. By 1800 the Spaniards were thoroughly rattled, because girls were already roaming the streets of New Orleans without chaperones and the way seemed clear for bordellos, boogie-woogie and the invention of Joe " King " Oliver by Jelly Roll Morton.* By this time it was perfectly obvious to the Spaniards that the French were the only people capable of handling a situation like this, so they persuaded Napoleon to take the place over again, lock, stock and barrel. Shortly afterwards the strain became unbearable and the French, having had word that the ubiquitous English were secretly making plans to move in and introduce Rugby football

* He also thought up Baby Dodds, the tailgate trombone, the upright piano, the inverted gas mantle, the Spanish tinge, the Mickey Finn, Hi-Fi, fried chicken, and W. C. Handy.

and other healthy games, cut their losses and sold the whole complicated mess to the United States for fifteen million dollars. This was called the Louisiana Purchase. It was effected in the Cabildo, on Jackson Square, New Orleans, where they now have on display a bronze mask of Napoleon pressed by his personal physician, with great presence of mind, forty hours after the Emperor's death (free, daily, 9 to 5).

As you might imagine New Orleans to-day is a pretty mixed-up sort of city. Apart from the Cajuns, the O'Reillys, and the Americans of African descent, there are the Creoles, who stem from the French and Spanish settlers, and the Americans, who drifted in to open drug-stores and betting parlours as soon as the dust settled. I had been advised not to miss the Audubon Park Zoo, but I'm no fool. I was in the French quarter (known as the Vieux Carré, after Carrie Nation) five minutes after my arrival, like everyone else. It is made chiefly of wrought-iron trellis work and looks Italian. I spent some time there, buying lace, and dropping in to the rowdy, smoke-filled little clubs to hear old cornet-players reminisce about how they taught Bunk Johnson to play, in the days when he still had teeth. I also went on a private tour of Storyville and downtown New Orleans, listening to the chugging of the Mississippi river-boats as I walked up Perdido Street into South Rampart Street, crossed into Basin Street, retraced my steps into Canal Street, turned left into Dauphine Street, turned right into St. Louis Street, crossed Bourbon Street, and so made my way down to Decatur Street, the docks, the levees and the river. My one regret was that I never found Beale street.*

But there is more to Louisiana then New Orleans. Who would have thought, for instance, that the State would contain four of the biggest salt mines in the world? Or that in the capital, Baton Rouge, they would still have the actual kettle in which the first granulated sugar was produced in 1794? How many of us realized that Huey P. Long's birthday is observed as a public State holiday because he built many fine roads, and probably made the trains run on time into the bargain?

The centre of the jumbo shrimp industry is at Morgan City, and there is plenty of other fishing along the coast, if you happen to be keen on giant jewfish, Spanish mackerel, tarpon, or the common jack. I also heard some talk of paddlefish, buffalo fish and fresh-water drum, but I preferred to spend my own evenings shooting coot, doves, foxes and gallinules in the bayous—those mysterious wildernesses of the swamplands, where the live oaks and cypresses

---

* Small wonder, really. No sooner had I got back to Euston Station than I remembered where it is. It's in Memphis, Tennessee, and all I saw there was a museum made of pink marble, at 275 Tilton Road.

are draped with Spanish moss, and alligators lurk among the cottonwood roots to bite your feet off at the first false move you make. The Spanish moss produces a most awe-inspiring effect, dripping and trailing from the huge, silent trees like some ghostly decoration, brushing with clammy fingers against your face as you move through the steamy inlets of the Mississippi. It is used for stuffing sofas.

Oh, a fascinating place—but time was pressing, and after a quick dash to Plaquemine to see the biggest chapel in the world small enough to hold only the priest and one slim acolyte during Mass, I moved on for a brief look at Tennessee.

It was disappointing. I got to Nashville, the capital, full of hope, for I had heard that it is famous for steel barges and clinical thermometers. Picture my dismay, therefore, when I was promptly rushed out to Centennial Park, and confronted with nothing less than the only full-sized replica of the Parthenon in the world!

" And what is more," they proudly told me, " this one's *cleaner*."

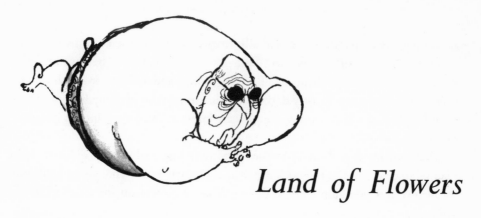

Land of Flowers

YOU might think there would be something special—something even awe-inspiring—about the moment when a man comes face to face with his first sausage tree. You might picture him sitting in his hotel room late the same night, trembling with a strange, inner excitement as he fills a page and a half of his diary with material of this kind:

Weather conditions good. To-day I had my FIRST GLIMPSE OF A SAUSAGE TREE. *How can I convey the magic quality of this chance encounter? Suffice it to say that life will somehow never be quite the same from this day on! Picture if you will, stark and proud against a gaudy background of etc., etc.*

It wasn't like that with me. " Get more aspirin," was all that I put in *my* diary, " and see about sailings for Southampton."

I hope I'm as thrill-hungry as the next man: no poker-faced sophisticate I, to pass a field of jet-black tulips or a brace of double-headed Skye terriers without so much as a piercing scream. But the fact is there is a limit, and I reached it—punch-drunk and slightly trampled-on—in a place called St. Petersburg, Fla. There was this sausage tree, and there I was standing before it, in the Sunken Gardens, hemmed in by a jostling crowd of bright-clad, sun-peeled, chunky-limbed amateur photographers in dark glasses. From all sides there came cries of well-fed astonishment, in a variety of regional accents, each tinged with an overtone of national pride.

" Holy cats, a sausage tree already! "

" Well, I do declare! Mervyn, will you look at that! "

" What exposure you got, Fred? "

" Landsakes, man, that's the *most!* "

And suddenly, as the myriad voices yelped and sang around me, I had had enough. My mind reeled with wonders: I was faint with an overdose of nature's marvels; giddy with the sight of elaborate fantasies dreamed up by cunning Man. After three weeks in Florida, the Land of Flowers, the Sunshine State, the playground paved with expense-sheets, cigar-bands and tote-tickets, what could a sausage tree possibly mean to me? Had I not already, not an hour before, seen actual shrunken heads in the St. Petersburg City Museum? Had I not been told that a local newspaper gives away one entire edition if the sun fails to appear before 2 p.m.? Had I not seen part of a mermaid through a glass-bottomed boat at Silver Springs, and touched the 1937 Mercedes-Benz for which the King of Afghanistan paid $40,000? Had I not heard a Bach Festival at Rollins College in Winter Park, after tramping up a Walk of Fame along which were stones taken from the birthplaces of six hundred bona fide World Personalities? Had I not hunted panther, wildcat and black bear, bathed in swimming-pools of filtered, scented sea-water, stood face to face with sooty tern and blue-faced booby on the Tortugas, and survived a six-day Shanty Boat Cruise up the Caloosahatchee River into Lake Okeechobee at a cost of $108 plus tax, with all meals and a swamp-buggy trip into the heart of a mangrove jungle, where I lost a monogrammed cigarette-lighter and met a Seminole Indian called Harrison, thrown in?

I had indeed: and I had done more. Even before I set foot in Florida I had flown hundreds of miles to the Badlands of North Dakota for breakfast, in a plane with running water owned by an Alabama cotton man. When he lived in North Dakota as a boy he used to like the way they fried eggs in a certain wayside diner near Medora (alt. 2,248 ft.). When we got there it was closed, and he wasn't too sure it was the right place anyway, so we flew to South Dakota. "I am a man of Quixotic whims," he said, as we flew across deep ravines, rugged terrain, unparalleled scenic wonders, mammoth formations, and grim masses of bare rock abounding in paleontological material of great interest, "and I have a notion that we should go down the Broken Boot Gold Mine."

This we did. The mine is in Deadwood, a pretty little place in the Black Hills, and we stayed there for three days on the off chance of striking a rich lode down some unfrequented side street. We failed in this, and as it was winter time we were also unable to see an entertainment called "The Trial of Jack McCall for the Murder of Wild Bill Hickok," which is staged in Deadwood five nights a week during the summer. This was one of the severest disappointments of my whole trip, only partly alleviated by my being shown Hickok's grave in the Mount Moriah Cemetery, together with those of Calamity Jane, Preacher Smith and Potato Creek Johnny. Jack McCall himself was hanged at Yankton. Whatever became of Deadwood Dick and Fly-Speck Billy I have so far been unable to ascertain.

Before leaving South Dakota, which is called the Sunshine State just like Florida, although I don't think they give many newspapers away, I insisted on visiting Mount Rushmore National Memorial, where a man* used to carve people's heads out of the solid granite of a mountain top.   Seeing that I was impressed by the sight, my host decided that we should fly slowly past the four gentlemen so grossly presented (they have heads between sixty and seventy feet long), and as he steered in close to Lincoln I saw him deliberately lean out of the cockpit and thumb his nose.

" You crafty old fox! " I cried, above the roar of the engines.   " It wasn't

* Gutzon Borglum.

94

fried eggs you came up here for at all!'' He only winked, and turned the plane's nose towards Alabama.

Certainly, I mused, political scars are not easily healed in this country.

It was immediately after this that I elected, of my own free will, to brave the Florida winter. When I tell you that Key West is the only city in the United States that never has frost, and that the guests in my Tallahassee hotel were requested not to remove their shirts in the dining-room unless a rocket was fired off in the gardens to signify that the air-conditioning had *actually broken down,* you will have some idea of the prevailing conditions. In one small town I slept with an electric fan in the bed, and on Thanksgiving Day in Tampa the raspberry ice-cream I was given with my Christmas pudding abruptly melted when a man at the next table lit a cigarette.

Because of my romantic and unquenchable appetite for the bizarre, the light-hearted, the quaint or the sentimental aspects of life in the twentieth century, I was particularly keen to inspect a turpentine camp; but for some reason I could find no one willing to take me to one. '' Look at it this way,'' they said, getting me into corners and lowering their voices. '' You're here to enjoy yourself, right? So why go around getting wrong ideas in your head about matters that are none of your damn business anyway, when you could be lying out on some beach with a cute doll and nothing to do but rub her back with sun-oil? Go to Miami,'' they said, '' and see the flamingoes.''

I went to Miami early in January. There was a temperature of 70 degrees on the day I arrived, but we also had a little precipitation: one point seven, to be exact—not enough to soak you to the skin, but a reminder just the same of the cruel forces nature has at her command. Miami consists of a seven-mile beach and nearly three hundred thousand people engaged in wheedling money out of the visitors, who love it. I stayed in a small hotel (fourteen storeys) crammed with beach photographers and their caption-writers. All night long the caption-writers would sit in the lounge, eating winter strawberries and composing their lyrical copy. '' *Brrr!!* '' they kept on writing. '' *Chilly? Not a bit, says curvy starlet Janice Pigalle, caught here by our candid cameraman as she emerges from a dip in the briny. But then, Janice is on location in far-off sunny Florida. Lucky Janice! Lucky cameraman! Lucky you!!* '' In the daytime I trudged about, moving an inch at a time, carried along in the endless crush of perspiring millionaires as they trod their weary pilgrimage of pleasure. With them I saw the Monkey Jungle, where the spectators stand in cages and the monkeys are guaranteed wild; the amphitheatre at Bayfront Park, which seats six thousand, but the show better be good; the Parrot

Jungle; the alligator-wrestling; the water-skiing; the jai alai; the coast-guards; and the Spanish Monastery, eight miles to the north, which was built in Segovia, Spain, in 1141, occupied by Cistercian monks, taken apart stone by stone on the instructions of William R. Hearst in the nineteen-twenties, shipped to the U.S. in ten thousand seven hundred and fifty-one crates, taken out of storage in 1951, and reassembled here stone by stone—painstakingly, and no doubt for a very good reason. (Adm. $1.30.)

Later, in Palm Beach, I found the older and less active millionaires. All is genteel and decorous here, for the quiet charm and tropical beauty of the place is jealously preserved. (Frinton comes to mind.) One proceeds sedately along Ocean Boulevard to one's private beach in one's Afromobile or bicycle-chair, and one sits under one's sunshade (or, at the first sign of precipitation, in one's rented cabana) wondering what those fiends back in Wall Street are up to, and whether they've found out yet that one's secretary *hasn't* gone to spend the winter with her Aunt Hattie in St. Paul, Minnesota.

I soon found that it is impossible to spend much time in Florida without entering into the carnival spirit. After a few days, therefore, having bought rope-soled shoes, a lemon-yellow play-shirt decorated with alternate gold and ultramarine beer cans, a Panama hat, Florida ankle-socks, Bermuda shorts, a Malacca cane, a Shantung beach coat, a Countess Mara tie and a pocket-size self-loading air-cooled colour cine-camera in Morocco leather case with built-in telescopic tripod and flash-bulb attachment, I lit a Havana cigar and plunged headlong into the social whirl. I will not pretend that the cute dolls flocked around me to any noticeable extent, because for one thing word quickly spread through the Florida grapevine that I always waited for my change from a fifty-dollar bill, and for another thing it must have been obvious from the start that the hired dinghy I had moored in the Yacht Basin at Daytona Beach was hardly adequate for champagne supper parties, let alone week-end trips to Cuba. None the less, I got about. I tried my hand at such vacation entertainments as skeet-shooting, shuffleboard and the judging of beauty contests. I visited the Seminoles in their straw huts deep in the shadowy Everglades, all among the palm trees, the water-lilies, and the powerful launches of the documentary-film makers. (These Seminoles refused to go to Oklahoma with the other displaced Indian persons in 1841, and have been hiding here ever since, not recognizing the U.S. Government and making their own separate declaration of war on Nazi Germany. They mostly hunt frogs.) I saw peat bogs and cement factories. I photographed pelicans, white ibis, egret, osprey, a titanium oxide works, and a three-

thousand-year-old cypress tree. I went to St. Augustine, the oldest city in the country, which, they assured me, was twice sacked by pirates: once by the English freebooter John Davis and once by Sir Francis Drake. This is a very lovely place, with overhanging balconies, grilled windows, patios, and a hum of Spanish guitars in the air.

Here I was able to see, in Potter's Wax Museum in the lobby of the Plaza Hotel, effigies of Babe Ruth, Joan of Arc, Harry S. Truman and many other notables—including a group showing Columbus making his dramatic appeal (rather curtly, it seemed to me) to Queen Isabella and King Ferdinand. These figures, they assured me, are the result of scrupulous research in the British Museum. As for the clothes, as I live and breathe they are the work of a costumier to the Court of St. James.

I saw the spring training quarters of the Detroit Tigers at Lakeland, the spring training quarters of the Brooklyn Dodgers at Wakulla Springs, the winter home of Harriet Beecher Stowe at Mandarin, the spring training quarters of the Cincinatti Redlegs *and* the Chicago White Sox at Tampa, and eight three-dimensional dioramas in the Stephen Foster Museum at White Springs, depicting his hit songs. (Free. Gift-shop. Parking 25c.) I made a tape-recording of a tobacco-auction at Live Oak. I backed six losers in a row at Hialeah. I was strapped into a boat and pulled three times round the Gulf of Mexico by a barracuda shark while my companions sat calmly slicing up bait in the stern and landing amberjack, dolphin, sailfish, kingfish, marlin, menhaden, wahoo, and cute dolls who had fallen overboard on account of being loaded. "Come to me, little fish," I kept whispering at the top of my voice. "I love you, little fish, and I'm going to get you alongside and chop off your great ugly head if it's the last thing I do, little fish." In the end I cut the line, and we had to get back to Key West under our own steam, just in time for a meal of Spanish limes, local gin, underdone turtle-steak smothered in conch chowder with sprouts and mashed potatoes on the side washed down with a glass of 99·9 per cent pure drinking water imported from Orange City, a medium portion of hot bollos, and a bowl of mixed pomegranates, sapodillas, papayas, quavas and celery.

All this, I tell you—and *then*, without warning, to be confronted by those ghastly sausage trees! I seem to remember that just before everything went black I pushed my way through the crowd and lashed out at the nightmare foliage with my cane. "I hate you, little sausage trees!" I cried. "I hope you die!"

They put it down to jealousy and carried me tenderly into somebody's hacienda to wrap me in wet towels.

And So Farewell

ON my way back to England I called in at the White House.

It was an informal visit—they were not even expecting me, as it turned out—but they very civilly offered to show me around, and it didn't cost me a cent. "I just happened to be passing," I said. "Please don't put yourselves out on my account." "Not at all," they said: "there are several other people here." While I was inspecting a four-pedestal Hepplewhite table in the dining-room, in company with two honeymoon couples and an outing of the Society for the Preservation and Encouragement of Barber Shop Quartet Singing in America, from Detroit, it occurred to me that I would probably have to give several days' notice before I could expect to do this kind of thing in Buckingham Palace, or even in Number Ten. The White House has a façade which reminded me very strongly of the Duke of Leinster's house in Dublin, and its history has not been without incident, as the following chronology will show:

1792. Cornerstone laid.

1800. The President's wife (a Mrs. Adams) hangs her washing in the East Room.

1814. The British do their best to burn down the whole building, after a portrait of Washington and other relics have been carefully removed and handed over to a Mrs. Madison (the President's wife).

1814. Madison moves to a house at 18th Street and New York Ave.

1817. Building restored, and painted white to hide the burns.

1935 (approx.). Lady secretary sees the ghost of Abraham Lincoln sitting on the edge of a bed pulling on his boots.

1947. Second floor porch added to south portico.

1948. One leg of a grand piano is observed to be projecting through the ceiling of the State Dining-room while the President's daughter (a Miss Truman) is upstairs getting in a bit of practice.*

1948.   Her father, who has suspected for some time that the house is on the point of falling to bits, tells Congress to fit a new interior at a cost of five and a half million dollars, and hotfoots it down the street to live at 1651, Pennsylvania Ave.

The White House, of course, is in Washington, the capital, which is in the District of Columbia, which is where part of Maryland used to be on the north side of the Potomac, except for a portion on the opposite bank, which is where part of Virginia used to be.   As if that weren't enough, the city, I was solemnly informed, is co-extensive with the District of Columbia, which may therefore be regarded as being largely mythical, and the maximum speed is 25 m.p.h.

Washington was laid out according to some rather fanciful designs dreamed up by a Major L'Enfant, an engineer who came over with Lafayette and distinguished himself during the planning of the city by demolishing a new manor house belonging to a wealthy landowner, who had refused to move it when told it would obstruct a vista.   Washington is thick with vistas, and has more trees than any other city in the etc., etc.   It is pleasant enough, but tends to be pervaded by a smell of red tape and sealing-wax.   It is populated chiefly by Civil Servants, official guides, postcard-sellers, and people connected with Security.

"If you should have occasion to telephone me," whispered a friend whose name I have since written on rice-paper and eaten, "don't for heaven's sake say anything vital, because everybody's wires are tapped, and the tappers' wires are counter-tapped, and brother is divided against brother, and there are men all over the place with powerful telescopes who can lip-read."

"Pull yourself together," I replied sharply.   "Take off that mask at once, and stop your melodramatic nonsense.   This is a public restaurant."

All the same, I'm bound to admit that as we rose to leave I distinctly heard the rustle of a shorthand notebook under the table: and half an hour later, when I slipped away from the main body during a guided tour of the Federal Bureau of Investigation in the Department of Justice Building (free), and wrenched open a steel filing cabinet labelled *Agents, Known, Red, Foreign-Born, with Characteristics, Distinguishing, and Operation, Mode of,* several uniformed guards moved me on quite openly, frowning.   But there it is: the Americans are extraordinarily touchy about such matters.

* She was pretty powerful in the left hand.

People come to Washington from all parts of the country, for all kinds of reasons. I stopped a good many of them in the street and questioned them closely. One had travelled fifteen hundred miles to complain to his Senator about a leaking roof. Another had just arrived from Idaho to see the arboretum in the Vanderbilt Mansion, and was greatly incensed when I told him it is in New York City, not far from Hyde Park. ("Well, I'll be gosh-darned," he said.) A man with a brown paper parcel told me he was going over to Herb's place to whoop it up a little. Eight different people said they were here partly on vacation and partly to check up on the Bill of Rights, the Declaration of Independence, the Andrew Mellon Collection, the first draft of the Gettysburg Address, the Gutenburg Bible, and the "Kitty Hawk." ("I visit them each and every year," one lady said, adjusting her scarf and speaking very distinctly. "In that way I renew my links with our glorious heritage and feel at one with the heroes of our past. Are we on the air at this very moment? Because if so I would like to say Hello to all at 174a Ojibway Drive, Ypsilanti, Michigan.) A grave, fattish person with a string tie and a black Stetson said he was on his way to the Senate Chamber, where he proposed to stand up in the public gallery and shower the members of Congress with privately printed leaflets urging the breaking off of diplomatic relations

with Haiti and an immediate reduction in the price of a monthly season ticket between Hoboken and Jersey City.

I left him on the steps of the Capitol, and wished him luck. The Capitol covers an area of three and a half acres, is situated at latitude 38° 53′ 22·9″ north and longitude 77° 00′ 33·7″ west from Greenwich, and is surmounted by a Statue of Freedom designed by F. Marion Crawford's father. A good deal of the routine work of governing the United States is carried on in these marble halls, and the country also has many conveniently situated golf courses. I asked the man on the door to give me a brief outline of the political system, and he explained that there are two parties—the Republicans, who stand for prosperity, peace, and a gradual emergence from the chaos left by the New Deal, and the Democrats (or '' those other bastards,'' as he put it), who stand for peace, prosperity, and a gradual emergence from the chaos left by President Hoover. It is open to any citizen aged thirty-five or upwards to become President, at a compensation of $100,000 a year, plus taxable expenses of $50,000, plus $40,000 for travelling and entertainment. The President's chief functions are to foster public relations by calling political correspondents by their first names at press conferences, and to decode or elucidate, for the benefit of the world at large, the policy speeches of his Secretary of State. It is a difficult job, and every four years the country is overrun with people declaring at the tops of their voices that they have not the slightest intention of standing for President. This is called campaigning.

While I was taking a sight-seeing stroll through the wide, airy streets of Washington, hearing the pulse-beats at the very heart of this diverse, rapidly-developing country, I began to feel already some of the pangs that were to grip me a week later, when I leaned over the rail of the promenade deck and watched the huts of the Brooklyn peasants fade gradually into the distance, merging at last with the horizon on the starboard side as I went below to make sure I'd packed those two towels from the Mayflower Hotel, Los Angeles. A feeling of nostalgia swept over me, misting my eyes as I stood bare-headed before the colossal statue of Lincoln (seated) in the Lincoln Memorial. '' Well, friend,'' I seemed to hear the old man sternly say, '' take home a good report. It is only through an accident of birth, remember, that you are not one of us: therefore do not reproach either yourself or us. And now move on and put away that hanky, for you're holding up the queue.''

I saw the old Ford Theatre, where Lincoln was shot while watching *Our American Cousin,* and the house in which he died, which covers an area of ·05 acres at 516 10th Street. I saw statues of Jefferson, Grant and Jackson, and learned that one statue of Grant is half an inch shorter than the statue of Victor Emmanuel in Rome. (I was able to find nobody who could account for this, although one elderly lady with a parasol suggested that Grant, a very cussed man, may have upset the arrangements by having his hair cut the day before the sculptor did his head.) I went up the Washington Monument in a lift (10c.) for a breath-taking view of the city and the Virginia hills, and came down by the stairs (free). I saw seven and a half million books in the Library of Congress, and a hundred-ton bronze reproduction of a photograph of the raising of the flag on Iwo Jima. I trotted through the Pentagon, which covers thirty-four acres, not counting sixty-nine acres for parking, and has a daytime population of twenty thousand, seventeen and a half miles of corridors, a ticket agency, a bank, a dental clinic, and a weekly consumption of forty thousand soft drinks. Exhausted at last, I collapsed on to a seat in The Mall, and presently a Representative came and sat beside me to ask my opinion of the first forty-five minutes of a filibuster he was preparing. " I'll stop 'em shipping small-arms and bubble-gum to those uncommitted hotheads in the Middle East,'' he said, " if I have to read 'em *The Brothers Karamazov* backwards! '' '' I'm afraid I know very little about politics,'' I said when I had heard him through, " but if I may hazard a suggestion, it seems to me that the whole thing would be vastly improved if you accompanied yourself throughout on the ukulele.''

His eyes lit up at once, and I am proud to think that as I sat there with him under the old shade trees, my American journey drawing to its close, I may have made my own small contribution to his nation's history.

It was the least I could do, for I had been shown much kindness in the U.S.A.* and seen great marvels. Later, in fact, as the mooring-ropes were cast off from our great ship, and the humble dock-workers joined hands on the quayside to sing their strange, haunting song of farewell, I realised that I had left out much from my record. Try as one will, some fleeting moments, seemingly unforgettable at the time, will inevitably elude one's pen in the rush of composition: and many of them came back to me then, while the fire-boats squirted me with water in the time-honoured way, and we nosed out of New York harbour into the grey wastes of the Atlantic. I smelt again the yellow jessamine fragrant on the evening air in Charleston, South Carolina, and the meat-packing plant at Orangeburg. I heard again the happy laughter on the campus of the University of Arkansas, where girls *and* boys receive

* On the comparatively few occasions when I was actually knocked down there were extenuating circumstances, such as bad light or an unfamiliarity with the language.

education at one and the same time.   I remembered the blonde who showed me round the dental laboratories at Milford, Delaware, and the brunette with whom I spent an interesting afternoon examining the Bancroft collection of pre-Raphaelite paintings in the Delaware Art Centre, Wilmington.   (Or was *that* the blonde?)   I recalled the wise old man I met on the beach at Ocean City, Maryland.   " Son," he said, gazing out across the calm waters of Sinepuxent Bay, " a country that has invented the cash register and the bifocal lens, the submarine and barbed wire, the Mason jar and the lawn-mower, the bottle-machine and the paper collar, safety pins and lightning rods, evaporated milk and the split-phase induction motor, is going to find an answer to it all *one* of these days, you see if it don't."   I remembered lazy days spent fishing on the Wabash, while the Hoosiers herded hogs along the valley.   Once more I roamed the rolling prairies of Iowa, rode the ranges of Western Nebraska with a bunch of daredevil cowboys and a certain Mrs. Olifant. Ah!—the Elk's Rodeo at Broken Bow!   Shall I, in some blazing August of the future, come back and guess the weight of that same cake, hear the thud of those pounding hooves, the fiddle's plaintive notes beneath the moon, the secret gurgle of the apple-jack . . . ?

Only in dreams, I fear.   It is not wise to return.   Things change.   What once was real and final can never be the same, will never be recaptured.

I stood at the rail and looked out over the restless, darkening ocean, until the pointing finger of the Statue of Liberty had sunk below the horizon, and America was once again a mystery, over the sea.   " O Captain!   my Captain! " I murmured with Walt Whitman, as I made by way back to my cabin—" O Captain!   my Captain!   our fearful trip is done."

Index

Date Due